Inanna's Ascent:
Reclaiming Female Power

a Girl God Anthology

Edited by Trista Hendren, Tamara Albanna
and Pat Daly

Cover Art by Arna Baartz

©2018 All Rights Reserved
ISBN 978-1720640615

All writings and art are the property of individual contributors. All rights reserved. None of the writings or artwork herein may be reproduced or utilized in any form or by any means, electronic or mechanical, including photocopying, recording or by any information storage and retrieval system, without prior written permission from the author or artist.

www.thegirlgod.com

Girl God Books

Original Resistance: Reclaiming Lilith, Reclaiming Ourselves

There is, perhaps, no more powerful archetype of female resistance than Lilith. As women across the globe rise up against the patriarchy, Lilith stands beside them, misogyny's original challenger. This anthology—a chorus of voices hitting chords of defiance, liberation, anger and joy—reclaims the goodness of women bold enough to hold tight to their essence. Through poetry, prose, incantation, prayer and imagery, women from all walks of life invite you to join them in the revolutionary act of claiming their place—of reclaiming themselves.

Re-visioning Medusa: from Monster to Divine Wisdom

A remarkable collection of essays, poems, and art: by scholars who have researched Her, artists who have envisioned Her, and women who have known Her in their personal story. All have spoken with Her and share something of their communion in this anthology.

Jesus, Muhammad and the Goddess

More than 35 international contributors reflect on finding Goddess within (and without) Christianity and Islam.

As I Lay by the Tigris and Weep

Poetry and musings by Tamara Albanna.

Hearts Aren't Made of Glass

My Journey from Princess of Nothing to Goddess of My Own Damned Life—a memoir of sorts by Trista Hendren.

How to Live Well Despite Capitalist Patriarchy

A book challenging societal assumptions to help women become stronger and break free of their chains.

The Girl God
A book for children young and old, celebrating the Divine Female by Trista Hendren. Magically illustrated by Elisabeth Slettnes with quotes from various faith traditions and feminist thinkers.

My Name is Medusa
The story of the greatly misunderstood Goddess, including why she likes snakes. *My Name is Medusa* explores the "scary" dark side, the potency of nature and the importance of dreams. Arna Baartz gorgeously illustrates this tale by Glenys Livingstone, teaching children (big and small) that our power often lies in what we have been taught to fear and revile.

My Name is Inanna
Tamara Albanna weaves the tale of Inanna's despair, strength and triumph—giving children of all ages hope that the dark times in life will pass. Arna Baartz illustrates this journey with gorgeous paintings of the owls, lions, stars, sun and moon that direct Her. *My Name is Inanna* is dedicated to Tamara's beloved homeland, Iraq—The Cradle of Civilization; the Land of the Goddess.

My Name is Lilith
Whether you are familiar with the legend of Lilith or hearing it for the first time, you will be carried away by this lavishly illustrated tale of the world's first woman. This creative retelling of Lilith's role in humanity's origins will empower girls and boys to seek relationships based on equality rather than hierarchy.

My Name is Isis
In this fresh look at the ancient Egyptian Goddess, Susan Morgaine reclaims Isis as The Great Mother Goddess and The Giver of Life, from whom all things come. Arna Baartz mystically illustrates Her as healer and protectress. *My Name is Isis* is a treasure box for children of all ages who want to draw close to this wise and nurturing Mother Goddess.

Complete list of Girl God publications at www.thegirlgod.com

Table of Contents

Introduction   1
Tamara Albanna

A Note About Styles and Preferences   4
Trista Hendren

Descent of the Dark Goddess for Personal Empowerment   5
Sofia Wren

For Inanna, Who cannot be Contained by a Grave   34
Amanda Lee Morris

Flight   36
Patricia Ballentine

Making Our Stand   37
Molly Remer

My Name is Inanna   46
Arna Baartz

I Can Hear Her   47
Annie Finch

The Song of Inanna   48
Liliana Kleiner Ph.D.

To Dance Her Seven Veils   54
Nuit Moore

Inanna's Ascent   58
Tara Reynolds

There's a Place for God, and It's in the Bedroom   59
Glenys Livingstone Ph.D.

Inanna Speaks   68
Molly Remer

Spirit Flight   70
Melissa Stratton Pandina

The Underworld   71
Talia Segal

Rising   74
Chantal Khoury

My Shoes   75
Lennée Reid

After the Descent   77
Tamara Albanna

Descent, Initiation and Return in The Syzygy Oracle   80
Heather Mendel

Myth as a Map to Healing and Wholeness   83
Heather Mendel

The Tree of Inanna   89
Liliana Kleiner Ph.D.

A Dive into Darkness to Become the Light   90
Jaclyn Cherie

Everyday Inanna   96
Molly Remer

I am a Priestess of the Goddess Patricia Ballentine	101
Strength from Shadow Susan Morgaine	103
The Descent Arna Baartz	105
Seeking Oracles Donna Snyder	106
Live by the Sun, Love by the Moon Carolina Miranda, OCT, M.Ed.	108
Inanna Advises Her Initiate Psyche North Torok	118
Shield For The Fiery Path Patricia Ballentine	119
Venus Direct as Inanna's Ascent: *The Empress Enthroned* Nuit Moore	120
Rising II Chantal Khoury	123
Inanna Lori Newlove	124
Shamans vs. Aliens: Adapting The Descent of Inanna K. A. Laity	125

Chaos and Creation — 129
Arna Baartz

We Were Inanna — 130
Hazel DaHealer

Ecstasy — 134
Iriome R. Martín Alonso

The Fuel of Life Itself — 135
Arna Baartz

Lily's Abortion in the Room of Statues — 136
Annie Finch

Everything Intensifies Me — 148
Benedetta Crippa

Inanna: Pregnant with Soul Voice — 150
Iyana Rashil

I Wear the Sun and Moon on my Crown — 158
Sinem Alev Koca

Daphne's Descent — 159
Daphne Moon

Seshat's Portal — 166
Patricia Ballentine

A Journey with Inanna — 167
Glenys Livingstone Ph.D.

The Magic Pouch — 173
Annelinde Metzner

Anonymous Art — 175

My Own Inanna: A Rebirthing — 176
Rev. DiAnna Ritola

Permission to Fall Apart — 181
Nina Erin Hofmeijer

Inanna's Ascent: Taking the Tough Love — 183
of the Shadow-Sister Back to the Light
Lyn Thurman

Reiki — 189
Melissa Stratton Pandina

Intention of Truth: My Journey Through — 190
the Underworld with the Dark Goddess
Genevieve Deven

Inanna of the Apple Tree, — 195
A Woman's Midrash to the Goddess
Hayley Arrington

Abundant Inanna — 198
Nuit Moore

Sacrifice to Sovereignty: — 199
A Healer's Real-Life Inanna Story
Melanie Miner

Of Ocean and Stars, Wildness and Sun — 209
Iriome R. Martín Alonso

Of Goddess' Nature: Balance — 210
Iriome R. Martín Alonso

Inanna Blue 216
Vicki Scotti

You Are Inanna 218
DeAnna L'am

The Sacred Marriage Text 221
Translated by Miriam Robbins Dexter Ph.D.

Madonna 222
Melissa Stratton Pandina

Seeking Sovereignty in the Land of the Dead 223
Carolyn Lee Boyd

Inanna, Above & Below 230
Laura Tempest Zakroff

Inanna in the Armenian Dance of the Reed 231
Laura Shannon

For my Dumuzi 247
Tamara Albanna

The Flight of Inanna 248
Liliana Kleiner Ph.D.

The Resurrection of Female Power 249
Trista Hendren

List of Contributors 260

*You've seen my descent
Now watch my
Rising.*

-Rumi

Introduction

Tamara Albanna

When we think of Inanna, she is usually envisioned as the descending Goddess—and often, it is her time spent in the Underworld that is most alluded to. While the Underworld, or the "shadow" is vital, it is equally important to remember what happens after the time spent in the darkness, the void, or the long dark tunnel.

Something wonderful happens—the caterpillar emerging from the chrysalis, the child leaving the womb, the flower bursting through the soil to bloom.

As you come out of that space, when things looked so utterly helpless at times, that's the "miracle" of the ascent, but it's not really a miracle at all, it's what comes next.

We are very much focused on the shadow. This is valid, and incredibly warranted, because not all is "Love and Light," all the time—that's just not realistic. One only has to turn on the news and see the intense darkness of this planet of ours. Balance is so desperately needed, but that balance works both ways.

Unfortunately, it seems as though the "shadow" has become somewhat commoditized, as with everything else that has a potential market in New Age circles. People realize the value, monetarily, of the shadow and shadow-work as it were.

Everywhere you turn these days there seems to be an obsession with the descent, and the darkness, as though we are somehow meant to spend a lifetime or two, in that space.

Even the title of this book, *Inanna's Ascent,* drew questions from those who thought Inanna is only about the descent. Have we not earned the emergence from darkness?

I descended from the Priestesses of Sumer—the keepers of Inanna's temple, during a time when the divine feminine was honored, and the name of the Goddess was on the tongue of all the inhabitants of the land. When the murderous patriarchy swept through, the civilization slowly began its descent, along with the Goddess—and all things feminine. Slowly, the Goddess was forgotten, and Her name became a distant memory.

The people of the land have suffered—particularly the women and girls—and although the Goddess is in their DNA, we are in need of a remembrance. Inanna descended, was killed, and re-emerged three days later—long before Jesus made that same journey.

Inanna descended for us, she was cleansed of her sins—and she cleansed us all as well—so why do we continue to suffer?

We descend our entire lives it seems—only coming up for brief moments of respite. Patriarchy pushes us down repeatedly—and sometimes, we just stay there.

When Al-Qaeda came into towns and raped women and girls en masse, we descended. When Daesh swept through the land, raped and murdered women and girls—while the world watched—we descended further and further. Wars, and sanctions, starvation and hopelessness—all by the patriarchal machine—we descended.

What is the response to this? In my view— and in the pages of this anthology as you will see— it is to remember. The beautiful women who have contributed to this work are all daughters of Inanna; they were all called home in one way or another. *Inanna's*

Ascent examines how women can rise from the underworld and reclaim their power through poetry, prose and visual art. All contributors are extraordinary women in their own right, who have been through some difficult life lessons—and are brave enough to share their stories.

Inanna is known as Queen of Heaven, but she really is a sexual Goddess. She is the very essence of woman—with divine spark in her womb: creation and destruction all at once. She chose her lovers, she did not allow a man to rule over her, and she knew her power. We are her daughters, and we have been silenced, made to feel unworthy, abused, hated, made to forget.

It is time to remember.

It is my hope that in the pages of this anthology, you too will remember, and begin your own journey—or continue the one you are currently on with renewed strength. My wish for you is to be the Goddess in your own life—to embody Her, and know your divinity.

For the women and girls of my Motherland, Iraq—the home of the Goddess, the cradle of civilization—may we rise again. May we once again turn to Her, and within ourselves, and remember who we are.

We have earned this ascent—all of us.

It is our time now.

A Note About Styles and Preferences
Trista Hendren

> "More than any other goddesses or god in the Sumerian pantheon, Inanna embodies the totality of "What Is." In that regard she represents the attempt of the Sumerian psyche to contain and to organize their apprehension of the chaotic, indecipherable, ineffable mystery of the known and unknown universe. She is their version of a personification of the whole of reality."
> -Betty De Shong Meador[1]

Inanna's Ascent contains a variety of writing styles from women around the world. Various forms of English are included in this anthology and we chose to keep spellings of the writers' place of origin to honor (or honour) each woman's unique voice.

It was the expressed intent of the editors to not police standards of citation, transliteration and formatting. Contributors have determined which citation style, italicization policy and transliteration system to adopt in their pieces. The resulting diversity is a reflection of the diversity of academic fields, genres and personal expressions represented by the authors.[2]

May the *Lady of the Largest Heart* speak to us all through Her daughters and return us to our birthright—grounded in Her reality.

---

1 Meador, Betty De Shong 2000. *Inanna: Lady of Largest Heart*. Austin: University of Texas Press.
2 This paragraph is borrowed and adapted with love from *A Jihad for Justice: Honoring the Work and Life of Amina Wadud*. Edited by Kecia Ali, Juliane Hammer and Laury Silvers.

Descent of the Dark Goddess for Personal Empowerment

Sofia Wren

Introduction

During the Fall of 2017, I felt a calling stir in me to talk about the Dark Goddess. I had received an invitation to speak to members of a nonprofit's leadership team because they wanted to serve more people from "untraditional spiritual paths." I'm someone who came from a "nontraditional" spiritual path, that is, I grew up with a secular anti-religious upbringing only to find inspiration from Goddess mythology and spirituality as a solitary practitioner, and later as a member of women's groups. So, there is much I could say about a voyage that began around age eight. In speaking about possible ways to conduct my talk with my advisor from the nonprofit, I found myself accepted with welcoming arms, but there was one snag. I felt the snag when I mentioned, "Hey wouldn't it be helpful if I mentioned the Dark Goddess? Some of my classmates at Loyola have found my perspective to be very interesting and enlightening." To the advisor, this was too advanced for the discussion, like a 300-level course when we were just at 101.

I accepted this in the moment, but as time passed and I returned home from the meeting I began to feel the rumble of various emotions and doubts. Was this limitation really fair? It struck a pang in me. Why was it not okay to talk about Her? This dark mother that holds me in the dark when I cry, so that I know it is OK? The one who understands the pain of abuse? Who feels my anger of being oppressed by forces and people in my life? Who wants to tear apart the broken systems and structures and start over from scratch? Who wants to punch back? Who knows my struggle to do the right thing when there are no clear answers?

Who knows the sorrow of grief and loss when it tears my heart apart? How could I hold in what I wanted to say about Her? It was a difficult rumbling. Over time, I came to agree with the decision that the explanation wasn't necessary for that particular forum. After meditating and rumbling, I decided to instead embody the energy of the Dark Goddess during my talk by going into my own personal darkness along my unique spiritual journey, speaking about when I was bullied and called a witch during middle school and as a result, shut down spiritually for ten years. But I knew I would be diving into the topic of the Dark Goddess more deeply soon, not only because of how passionately I felt about the topic's significance, but also because of what happened the same week.

That very same week, a few days after the conversation with my advisor, I attended a group called Full Circle at the Unitarian Universalist Church of Annapolis (UUCA). It's an open earth-based, spiritual women's circle I've attended over the course of many years, which has different themes for different meetings. I didn't know the meeting topic until I walked into the door, and behold my surprise when it was the Dark Goddess. In all my years of attending, I'm not sure we've ever had a richer group discussion. Somewhere between ten to fifteen women attended the meeting, and every woman had something to say about how she connected to the Dark Goddess for deep benefits to her own life. While for people who are not familiar with the Dark Goddess, it may seem "out there" or intense or very far along the path (and, no, it's not evil). However, from what I heard and took away from the night's discussion, it seemed to me that working with "dark" aspects of Goddess, divine feminine energy or feminine archetypes is more prevalent and less unusual among those women called to earth-based, neopagan or spiritual practice than I would have thought. In fact, considering the relative diversity and eclectic nature of the women involved in my group, it actually seemed one of the few things we could all agree on beyond appreciating nature and the elements. We nibbled on dark chocolate and sipped little cups of red wine as we talked into the night about our lives, the Goddess, and her journey descending into and ascending from the underworld. To me this was a sign; there was something here, something more.

As my Masters in Spiritual and Pastoral Care at Loyola University Maryland rounded to a finish in the Spring of 2018, it seemed obvious to me what I would write about for my final thesis: the Dark Goddess, the one who descends into the underworld, and how to take the work with Her deeper. Given the depth of the discussion from my women's group Full Circle at the UUCA, I was led through the thesis guidelines to conduct a thought experiment about what "taking it deeper" in that context might truly mean. I had to explain the Dark Goddess in layman's terms so to speak: taking the explanation to the higher level I didn't get a chance to explore before. To do so, I describe the Dark Goddess as an archetype rather than just a deity. Some people will see it differently, but I'm flexible; whether the divine is a part of my consciousness or external is not something I quibble about because to me All is One and it is all the same. I am divine and powerful, and so is Goddess, God and all the rest. By focusing on archetypes, I hoped to explain in the clearest of terms and be as inclusive of those in my community as possible—as some are atheist or agnostic.

At the end of preparing the original paper I also proposed a group of 6-8 sessions as a possible way to take this work deeper. The women's group I proposed is a sacred space with different introspective activities and discussion to explore collectively this descent into the underworld modeled on the Dark Goddess' journey based on mythology. The descent is to result in a new ascent with <u>more pleasure, more power, more depth and richness in life than ever before.</u> When we are truly awake, there is a richness and beauty to life that we couldn't see before, and the journey of the Dark Goddess honors the natural cycles of inner healing. Sometimes you need to go through the fire, into the dark, through the shit, only to come out stronger and lighter than ever before. I hope to facilitate a women's group like this in the future, whether it is at the UUCA, another Unitarian church, a spiritual center, or through Zoom online. I'm open to whatever the future will bring! I chose not to include any more of my thesis beyond this chapter for brevity's sake, but I can be contacted for more information.

Meanwhile, it behooves me to say that I'm always doing my own work. I am not immune. The Goddess has taught me to be willing to descend below so that I may joyfully embrace life each day. It is these journeys that have changed my life, doing the difficult thing, facing emotions or parts of myself that are hard to look at, saying the things and doing the things that I feel called to, even though I do not want to. Never before in my life have I been so willing to listen. During this final semester of grad school, I not only wrote this paper, but I flung open the doors of my life. I moved out of the apartment I lived in with my previous partner of seven years at New Years. Recently in June, I was visiting my old house to cry together over our fur-baby, my childhood cat, who then passed away. For the last six months, I struck out on my own, free of student loan or parental support, and juggled all my talents to make a living. I embraced my abilities as a massage therapist and healer, while being more discerning in my freelance writing, editing and coaching business. I began to prepare to leave life as I know it with the acquisition of a job teaching English in Japan in 2019.

I have seen the ways my personal hell seems to repeat itself in my romances, and have let patterns go. Much as I'd like to focus on the other areas of my life, The Dark Goddess would have me say that often my romantic life takes up the biggest focus of my energy and it has always been that way. I love people on such a deep level—like all people no matter what. If you were like that, imagine how difficult it would be to lose the love you build your days on, and then imagine finding out, that as much as you'd prefer another life partner, that it's also okay to love people in other ways, too. I've had my share of heartbreak in the past and these days I'm more aware of the losses while at the same time I am grateful for everything that I've got. Trust me, it's not all bad. I'm single again after seven years, and I compare myself now with who I used to be before. I've grown.

I'm stretching my ability to receive, as well as my ability to let go. I have a lot to learn, but I'm learning. Goddess will teach me more, I assure you. A wise man knows he is a fool: A quote that's served as a mantra to me considering my name means wisdom. I have begun seeing myself as a leader or a teacher, but at the same time I am just a vessel for something larger.

The requirements of being Her Priestess are exacting, but there is no turning back now. I only aim to follow the guidance as best I can. I know I am a Goddess, and my Goddess guides me—even when it is difficult, and even when it is hard. This is path to the easiest brightest future—leaving the parts of me behind that do not help me grow. I release who I think I am every day and empty to what is truly inside of me.

The worst of this particular journey is over. Today I feel like I have ascended, but one day I will go down deep again. I still take day trips to the underworld regularly. And so I shine with the light of day, brighter than I am used to. Now I know myself, including the sadness, the fear, the pain, the heartache, the sexuality, the neediness, the strength, the anger, the wisdom, the gift of me. Truly, despite the challenges, I'm not sure life has ever been this good. Thank you, Goddess.

Selection from Chapter II of Sofia Wren Nitchie's Thesis, "Exploring a Deeper Connection to the Dark Goddess for Personal Empowerment"

During the November meeting of Full Circle at the UU Church of Annapolis, women shared how working with the Dark Goddess gave meaning to their lives. In order to explore how this theme may be explored more deeply within the same church community to support women more, this chapter will explore the meaning of the Dark Goddess and why it is important for a future event to happen at the Unitarian Universalist Church of Annapolis or in another venue.

Introduction to Archetypes by Carl Jung

What is the Dark Goddess? The Dark Goddess is an archetype. Carl Jung introduced the term archetype into psychology and was an important contributor to the development of the concept (Craighead & Numeroff, 2004, p. 81). Included in this concept is Jung's understanding of the unconscious, as having two layers— one is personal, based on the individual life experience of a person, and one is the collective unconscious. The collective unconscious contains archetypes, or "primordial images that have existed from the remotest times, but images that lack clear content" (p. 81). The content of those images is based on the personal experience of symbols and images. Jung considered the archetypes to be fundamental to the psyche: "They are forms that underline everything we perceive, imagine, and think" (p. 81). His understanding of archetypes was based both on Jung's self-exploration and philosophical conception, as well as empirical research with psychotic patients who shared common patterns of images and symbols which they could not have learned from experience and thus must have pulled from some collective unconscious (p. 82). There are many other archetypes or characters which are commonly recognized, such as the Hero. The author considers the Dark Goddess to be a separate archetype.

The Feminine Shadow or Darkness

Jung also describes some aspects of our behavior, intellect or perception as associated with the shadow (Craighead & Nemeroff, 2004, p. 82). These are things that we do not have much conscious control over. He also describes the animus and anima. A man will have feminine qualities that he cannot realize consciously within himself, and this is called the anima. Similarly, a female will have unrealized masculine qualities within herself, called the animus. These different concepts of a shadow side held within each person are connected to the idea of a Dark Goddess.

For the purposes of this paper, the Dark Goddess is an archetype that, under the intention of a benevolent group like Full Circle, does not mean harm, but who embodies shadow aspects, including feminine power that lies within every woman, or specifically the women in the group. She is a Goddess rather than a God, because she is an archetype that is present within the female participants in the group and connects to what power could look like for these women. In striving to find a personal fit for what power could look like for them in their lives, she would be helpful. If this were a men's group, perhaps a Dark God might be more appropriate to tap into the shadow of the male participants, but Full Circle is a women's group so this paper is focused on the Dark Goddess. She is not evil or malicious, although she may exhibit uncomfortable qualities or be connected to uncomfortable emotions. Because she is divine, power is naturally one of her traits, including power that women have not been able to activate consciously. The Dark Goddess is an important archetype that resonated with all the women who attended the November meeting, and furthered a rich discussion which could be expanded upon in another future event.

The feminine Darkness or Shadow includes a diversity of things. In the womb of the Goddess, all things are sacred and perfect, including shadow and light, which were all created for a purpose. Within the conversations held at Full Circle, women discussed a connection between the Dark Goddess and emotions such as anger, self-pity, blame, or shame. The shadow can include these uncomfortable and difficult-to-control emotions. Another aspect of the shadow could be anything that an individual woman or women collectively were taught to suppress. This could be parts of the self, like behaviors, thoughts, emotions, that society or a person's environment consider to be inappropriate for that woman to experience or express. For instance, women in the Full Circle group discussed saying 'no' and having boundaries as difficult because it was taught to them to try to work well with others and say 'yes.' Something about saying 'no' and holding boundaries was difficult to express and in the shadow, and for many women in the group, some part of saying 'no' may still be in darkness to create an ongoing struggle through life. If something was taught to be inappropriate to an individual woman or women generally—like saying 'no'—then that individual will learn to adapt to their environment by placing this aspect or archetype of themselves in the shadow or darkness. Debbie Ford (1998) describes a metaphor created by John Welwood where each person begins life with a brilliant mansion of rooms full of light, which they can traverse at will any time they like (p. 26). Each room represents a way of being or acting, different aspects of the Self. At first there is no shadow or darkness anywhere in this house of light, nor in any of the rooms. As she or he grows, the child begins to learn that exploring certain rooms results in a negative consequence from their caretakers or others in their environment. Perhaps it does not help them to win love or gain rewards, or perhaps they are told it is not meant for them, or perhaps they see that exploring those rooms results in suffering or punishment. They take this experience and learning and decide to put the light out in the rooms they see as creating those negative consequences, until their mansion is full of dark windows, with some in light. This can occur as a conscious act or this turning off of the light can be a subconscious reaction to what is going on in their life and the meaning that they make out of it.

Becoming aware of one's shadow can assist in one's personal growth. Jung describes a process called individuation. In individuation an individual becomes conscious of the contents of the collective and personal subconscious so it can be integrated into the personality (Craighead & Nemeroff, 2004, p. 82). The author connects this concept to what Maslow termed as self-actualization, "the need for inner satisfaction from life as a whole and the search for fulfillment of the needs for satisfaction in life experience" (p. 86). The exploration of the shadow can not only free one up to new possibilities of being, but perhaps there is value inherent in simple conscious awareness for the purposes of individuation. Women in the Full Circle meeting in November were able to connect to the Dark Goddess archetype—and shared meaningful connections in the discussion. The Dark Goddess connected them to empowerment, self-worth and better boundaries. Further exploration of the Dark Goddess in future events at the UUCA or online could have benefits that help the women there to pursue self-actualization.

Female Oppression and Darkness

Feminism teaches that women as a group face certain kinds of patterns in their oppression; this can in turn can illuminate patterns among women that could connect to a shared darkness. This means that groups of women may be able to relate to one another in discussing the Dark Goddess and their darkness, including the difficulties of their lives, where they are held back or trying to grow and how their lives have been driven by a need to not be certain ways. Perhaps these interconnections due to gender-based oppression are a part of why the discussion during the original Full Circle meeting was so rich. Discussions of feminism have been a part of Full Circle events in the past and could be expanded in other events carrying the themes of the Dark Goddess forward. Although experiences will vary from person to person, especially in light of class, race, culture, or sexual orientation differences, if women as a whole have not been empowered by the patriarchal systems, then aspects of their power will be in the shadow. Men also experience oppression, but perhaps their experience is different, which is part of why women benefit from discussing their lives in single gendered environments like Full Circle.

Empowerment is a large theme for the Dark Goddess. The concept of empowerment is conceptual and one definition used by developmental economists is that it is, "a process of 'undoing internalized oppression,' and therefore, when focused on women, it involves changing the social and cultural norms inherent in patriarchy that sustain women's subordination. It has similarly been argued that empowerment increases a woman's sense of agency or what has been termed as 'power within'" (Paludi & Grabe, 2010, p. 23).

Strength, as well as weakness can be in the shadow for individual women, and be a topic explored in a future event for Full Circle. Since masculine forms of strength seem more dominant throughout our culture to the author, this leads to a conclusion that aspects of strength that are more authentic to women, but less culturally recognized, and may be in the shadow for women. Because strength is culturally seen in America as a desirable quality over weakness, then feeling weak would also be in the shadow. So, both feminine power and weakness can lie within the shadow. In discussion of the Dark Goddess, Full Circle members talked about processing pain, grief, loss and feeling bad about themselves while feeling the presence of the Dark Goddess— while also connecting her to the power to say 'no' or strength to defend oneself from an attack. Although these themes of weaknesses and strengths may on their face seem radically different and perhaps random or incompatible, the shadow could include both these themes. The shadow aspects which were not integrated by women into their consciously controlled and socially acceptable personality include both sides of the spectrum of power and weakness. This could also create a tension or dilemma where women must find a very fine line of balance.

Collective shadow aspects for women can be in the form of a false paradigm or tension of opposites. An example of this tense dichotomy and challenge to women is the well-known "Virgin-whore" or "Madonna-whore" split. Although, in actuality, a woman can be both sexual and proper, especially at different times in her life or even at the same time, this false paradigm creates a sense that a woman has to be careful of being too sexual or not sexual enough. The old problem is around acceptance by society, where a woman does not want to appear to be too sexual, nor be too absent of sexual attractiveness or frigid, as both would repel a man.

This duality is difficult because it makes it hard for women to feel safe no matter what she does in her sexuality. A woman in danger, could be accused of appearing as either from shadow sexuality, virgin or whore. Of course there are other options, but the illusion being perpetuated is that things are black and white. This false paradigm limits a woman's options severely and even creates a situation where she is probably going to be vulnerable to feeling shame no matter what she does. She cannot win. There is a fragile space in which she can be experiencing herself or be seen by others as in the Light, and so many other thoughts, feelings, and behaviors may lead her to explore a shadow place. Women are vulnerable to shame depending on external feedback. If that external feedback is negative, then experiencing that shame or admitting she has these experiences, thoughts or desires outside of what is acceptable by society can be a harmful experience. There are so many opportunities for a woman to feel shame and uncomfortable feelings due to oppression. Perhaps the only solution is not to play the game, and to choose to step into the Shadow willingly rather than wait to be pushed into it from an outside force as victim. As women discussed their connection to the Dark Goddess in the Full Circle group, they were able to question messages and false paradigms of society so that they could heal. Discussing society-wide paradigms and expectations or limits for women could be a way to bring richness to Full Circle events in the future.

Not everything in the shadow is bad—there is actually strength in the shadow. This is one of thought leader Debbie Ford's (1998) main messages, "It is not just our denied 'darkness' that finds its way into the recesses of our shadow. There is a 'light shadow,' a place where we have buried our power, our competence, and our authenticity" (p. 19). As mentioned before, if women have not been able to access a conscious control over inner strength or other positive qualities in their lives, then these qualities may remain in the shadow. One of the other benefits of working with the shadow is also to expand personal freedom and choice. "Freedom is being able to choose whoever and whatever you want to be at any moment in your life. If you have to act in a particular way to avoid being something you don't like, you're trapped. You've limited your freedom and robbed yourself of your wholeness" (Ford, 1998, p. 19). One obvious way of looking at this is that everything a person has not achieved yet—their true potential—must be in the shadow if it has not yet come to light. The highest level of brilliance, power, beauty, charisma, intelligence, achievement and so forth is within a person already, yet outside of one's ability to consciously tap into it because it is in the shadow. The Goddess within every woman has one foot in the shadow. On another level, every aspect of a human being is neutral and is only bad in light of how it is used. For instance, if a person is inclined to be angry and yell, this may be helpful in order to guide a child who has run into the street to never do that again. Or perhaps being angry and yelling would be a helpful response to an attacker or trespasser. In that case perhaps a problem would occur for a person who tried very hard not to be angry and yell in their life because they had suppressed that kind of behavior and it became a shadow aspect. Although being angry and yelling may not seem to be "light" qualities, they could be helpful in certain situations. Or there may be emotions in the shadow that are difficult to access because they are not appreciated by society—such as disenfranchised grief. Although tapping into those feelings might be very uncomfortable and feel very dark, the author knows that it can also be very beautiful to finally mourn the losses and feel the emotional pain.

The Dark Goddess archetype involves more than a connection to difficult emotions such as anger, weakness or depression. She can also encompass great joy, pleasure, power, value and the joys of receiving rather than simply giving and giving. Through personal experience and working with women as a life coach for many years, the author observes that sometimes receiving can be more difficult than giving. Financial inequality can be an example of this theme. Women are still receiving less money per hour on average than men, despite doing more work when home care is included. "Census statistics released on August 26, 2008 Women's Equality Day, indicated that average, full-time employed women earn 77.8 cents to every dollar earned by full-time employed men... Furthermore, this wage gap is more severe for women of color." (Paludi & Grabe, 2010, p. 147-148). The book *Women Don't Ask* details multiple studies to suggest that women are less likely to ask for raises and thus do not get them, beginning with their own inability to take steps to request more pay (Babcock & Laschever, 2007). The author believes that many women do not allow themselves to receive positive feeling states because they have been acculturated to be care providers, to remain agreeable, or because they feel unsafe receiving or feel unworthy of receiving. It may feel safer for women to pursue deserving goodness or earning it, through such things as waiting for a boss to give her a raise rather than asking for it. In waiting for a raise, a woman would be releasing power to create positive changes on her own and depending on an outside authority to recognize her talent. Depending on an external authority for validation, praise or positive rewards—like waiting for a raise that may never come independent of a request—could result in disappointment and pain, which could lower one's self-worth and positive feeling. Further work around the Dark Goddess at the UUCA could help women to feel more comfortable asking others for raises and rewards and enjoying good things in their lives to a greater degree.

During discussion at Full Circle, many women connected working with the Dark Goddess to personal worth. The Dark Goddess themes could help women to see their inherent worth more. There is a difference between earning positive rewards from an outside source and enjoying oneself as a child of God. Wiccans often cite the scripture of the *Charge of the Goddess* by Doreen Valiente, where the Goddess speaks to say, "All acts of love and pleasure are my rituals. Let there be beauty and strength, power and compassion, honor and humility, mirth and reverence within you." There is research looking at women's journals from the American witch trials detailing how women were more likely to believe that they were wretches or unworthy of God's love, which could explain why women more than men confessed to capital crimes of witchcraft (Reis, 1999, p. 15). This serves as a striking example of how women are often hard on themselves and feel unworthy of divine love and good things; in this case worthiness would be in the shadow for them to explore. Working with the Dark Goddess, women such as those in Full Circle can access more goodness in their lives through deeper work with these themes.

Self Oppression

In feminist theory, one important analogy is that of the birdcage (Frye, 1983). Patriarchal patterning creates mental frameworks and schemas that guide certain ways of thinking. The feminist thought leader Frye has noted that these frameworks cage and limit the ways that women operate from the inside out. These oppression-related ways of thinking entrap a woman in her own mind and form bars similar to that of a bird cage--a sense of being externally being watched in a prison from a guard tower (panopticon) that can monitor prisoners' activity in every direction, to the effect that even when no one is watching, a prisoner will tend to monitor themselves and enforce rules on themselves as if they were being watched all the time anyway. (Foucault, 1995).

This is an analogy of what oppression does in a society—it forces women to become their own prison guards. In order to find empowerment and freedom from patriarchal oppression, a woman must free her mind from the modes of thinking put on her. These bars, however, are invisible—and to begin the process she must be aware of them first (the most difficult step), take responsibility for the way she is limiting her own self (not always easy considering the unfairness of being blamed for her own misfortune under oppression), and then she must remove the bars (also difficult). The environment inside of the birdcage or the prison, what a woman is used to, is in the Light, and the free, wide area of freedom surrounding her limited environment of the birdcage or the prison is actually her Shadow or Darkness.

A phrase that comes to mind in describing the Shadow for a woman, are the places where she might be invited and instead say, "OH I could never do that," or "That's not for me. I'm not like that," or "I don't like women who are like that." These places, actions, beliefs, feelings, or ways of being are not just restricted to her from society or external forces—they are places she will not allow *herself* to go, which is the ultimate form of oppression and the most difficult to remove because they hinge on her own awareness and free will in addition to the complex healing of the traumas, learning, or oppression that created this pattern.

Some may even criticize aspects of psychology and the way psychology is understood to further continue the limited frameworks of the patriarchy, creating more questions for how one can extract herself. Pollock and Turvey-Sauron (2007) wrote that:

> "Many scholars have noted with perplexity the deeply archaeological Freud's cursory attention to any evidence from the ancient worlds he collected of non- and pre-patriarchal cults and their imaginary foundations. The way in which the maternal-feminine thus appears even in psychoanalysis is marked by the patriarchal, familial economy, and the social structure of modern (i.e., post-classical) European man's worlds. Degradingly animalized, deprived of all rights over the very body that makes life, forced into domestic servitude, sexually policed and repressed, denied the very dignities of her human sisters, intellectually, materially and emotionally impoverished, often physically brutalized and even mutilated in the service of her patrilinerarity, the maternal-feminine is made cruelly into the other, thing, meaningless…. But how do we get beyond the binary terms in which the patriarchal economy and patrilineal thought imprisons us?" (p. 30).

If a woman's interaction with the helping profession of psychology may possibly be within the frameworks of the patriarchy, how can she extract herself? Accessing the spirituality of the Dark Goddess in a supportive group may be one way to expand a sense of consciousness and thus transcend the limitations of both self-imposed and collective oppression.

The Hero's Journey and the Dark Goddess Journey

The Hero's Journey made famous by Campbell (2008) describes a narrative repeated across cultures where a man ventures into the world, goes against challenges, and overcomes evil in some fashion, to return home and give the gift of his labor to his people so that they may grow. In contrast, the author's understanding of Dark Goddess journey is not a linear journey outward into the world, but a voyage inward, to the depths or into death itself. Several sources argue that the Hero's Journey is supported by patriarchal culture because it encourages the archetypal Son to create as much distance and separation as possible between himself and his mother to form a distinctive identity so that the Mother is Other.

In some cases, there is an incest theme in the old myths. Pollock (2007) writes that, "Death and incest... form the dominant issues not at the level of imagining sex with the mother, but as a rule to ensure the proper distance and separation between Mother/Son" (p. 34). She references Harrison who considered Mother/Son the foundational pair of all creation, "not as sexual, relational pair, but a pairing of symbolic entities of the creative Mother and the blossoming, new rod or branch of resurrected annual fertility; the Son's son-ness is the sign of his youth and seed-bearing." The son is "figuration of the concept, Spring, to the Mother as duress, time and continuity, the seasonal cycle and the cycle of life and death" (p. 34). Exploring different kinds of myths in sacred community can help women explore new possibilities for their lives and relationships.

The scholars who discuss Goddess myths imply that there is value in seeing a distinct goddess journey as a possible source of guidance for women. Since Campbell (2008) believes that myths guide people to becoming the best versions of themselves individually and collectively, having a guiding myth for women to build on in their lives and discuss with others can be an extremely valuable experience. Myths can be seen as scriptures as well. During the Full Circle meeting, the women discussed myths of the Goddess. These themes or even a discussion of the differences between Hero's Journey and a Goddess journey can be a part of group discussion for a future Full Circle event.

Dark Goddess Myths

Myths can be scriptures to those in the Wiccan, pagan and earth-based communities. During the regular monthly Full Circle meetings, women often share the oral telling of ancient myths and discuss their meaning. Looking specifically at myths about the Dark Goddess, this archetype includes the story of Persephone discussed during the November Full Circle meeting. Persephone is daughter of Demeter from ancient Greek mythology. Demeter is the goddess of the grain, and as the story goes her daughter is picking spring flowers when Hades, lord of the underworld, snatches her, as it is often told, rapes her, and brings her into his realm beneath the Earth (Gadon, 1989, p. 192). Here she is brought under the earth, forcibly, for an adventure in which she is not allowed to go home for some time. Demeter is grieving and angry, and punishes the earth with famine and drought in her pain. Both Persephone and Demeter show aspects of the Dark Goddess—in one, the intense experience of not having sovereignty or dignity of one's body as victim, and the other angry grieving and the merciless punishing of innocent parties for her pain (p. 195). Finally, Zeus, king of the Gods ruling from the sky, responds to Demeter's behavior to release Persephone because he knows that making her happy will establish the fertility of earth and produce food again.

However, in the common modern day telling, Hades has already tricked Persephone into eating six tiny pomegranate seeds, and so she may only return to her mother on earth for six months out of the year and is required to return to Hades for the other six months. This is how we have winter and summer according to the myth. In this basic myth, darkness is involved in the adventure into the underworld and it restricts Persephone's access to light, freedom, her mother's love and the greater world.

In some tellings popular at Full Circle's women group, the story is told differently so as to empower the Goddess Persephone. Perhaps Persephone actually wanted to explore her independence and a sexual relationship with Hades, who did not rape her, and choose to become his queen by choosing intentionally to eat six seeds. If Persephone is not raped but instead consciously chooses a relationship with Hades, the tale is more empowering. It would also involve Dark Goddess aspects of daring to choose her own path, even if it pushed back against expectations that she should remain with her mother rather than being a sexual woman claiming a seat of royal power in the underworld through a relationship with Hades the king.

In class discussion at Loyola, this tale was discussed as similar to some retellings of Adam and Eve (Thomas Rodgerson, personal communication, November 27, 2018). Rather than being a source of sin, perhaps Eve was daring and powerful to eat the apple from the tree of knowledge and create opportunities for humankind to experience their own meaning-making in the world. This myth is a script that can be used to understand aspects of the Dark Goddess theme, and its interpretation to be more empowering shows the values of the Full Circle group towards empowerment.

Another important Dark Goddess myth or scripture is the Tale of Inanna. The myth about Sumerian goddess Inanna is the oldest known myth of the descent of the goddess (Perera, 1989, p. 9). She is a sky goddess, queen of heaven and fertility goddess; extremely powerful in many ways in her time. As the story goes, Inanna ventures into the underworld willingly to witness a funeral of Gugalanna, husband of Ereshkigal. But in doing so, she enters the territory of another divine queen, that of the underworld and therefore must submit to her power. As queen of the Great Below, Ereshkigal is furious and demands that Inanna follow the rules for all who enter her realm, and be brought "naked and bowed low" (p. 9). As she descends through the seven gates, one-by-one her magnificent regalia and jewelry are removed, and she is judged by seven judges. Ereshkigal kills her and hangs her corpse "on a peg, where it turns into a side of green, rotting meat" (p. 9). Eventually her handmaiden is able to appeal to Enki, the god of waters and wisdom who rescues her, "using two little mourners he creates from the dirt under his fingernail." They slip unnoticed into the Netherworld, carrying the food and water of life with which Enki provides them, and they secure Inanna's release by commiserating with Ereshkigal... She is so grateful for the empathy that she finally hands over Inanna's corpse," (p. 10) and Inanna is restored. This myth can be one used for future discussion in groups or events at the Unitarian Church and also lends itself to the topic since it has been analyzed by Jungian psychologists.

Interpretations of the Inanna Myth

Perera (1989) offers four interpretations of the Inanna myth (p. 13). The first involves a connection to the rhythms of nature which include a "dwindling and replenishing of the storehouse" (p. 13). Her descent and death can be similar to winter, while the rise is similar to spring and summer. The connection to the seasons is also evident in the myth of Persephone as her mother mourns her absence each year and creates winter. The cycle of nature and representation of the Goddess during the dark time of the year was also discussed during the Full Circle ceremony occurring in November. November is part of the dark time of the year when the earth is slowing and the leaves have fallen. This time of year may be perfect for another cycle of events on the theme of the Dark Goddess.

Perera's second interpretation is that of an initiation process into the mysteries. Inanna's path into the underworld presents a "paradigm for the life-enhancing descent into the abyss of the dark goddess and out again. Inanna shows us the way, and she is the first to sacrifice herself for a deep feminine wisdom and for atonement. She descends, submits, and dies. This openness to being acted upon is the essence of the experience of the human soul faced with the transpersonal. It is not based upon passivity, but upon an active willingness to receive" (p. 13).

In discussing the initiation process in Western tradition, Perera distinguished between this initiation process of the Dark Goddess and other modes which may be more related to the Hero's Journey. She noted that initiation involves "exploring different modes of consciousness and rediscovering the experience of unity with nature and the cosmos that is inevitably lost through goal-directed development. This necessity—for those destined for it—forces us to go deep to reclaim modes of consciousness that are different from the intellectual "secondary process" levels the West has so well refined. It forces us to the affect-laden, magic dimension and archaic depths that are embodied, ecstatic and transformative; these depths are preverbal, often pre-image, capable of taking us over and shaking us to the core. In those depths we are given a sense of the one cosmic power... On those levels the conscious ego is overwhelmed by passion and numinous images. And, though shaken, even destroyed as we knew ourselves, we are recoalesced in a new pattern and spewed back into our ordinary life... Connecting to these levels of consciousness involves a sacrifice of the upper-world aspects of the Self to and for the sake of the dark, different, or altered-state aspects" (p. 14). These themes may be relevant to a further discussion group or activity on the theme of the Dark Goddess for the Unitarian Church or at another venue.

Perera's third interpretation is that the myth is a description of the pattern of psychological health for the feminine. She describes the healing process as similar to a descent and releasing of layers of the self. This process may be one that could be included in some kind of event at the church. Her fourth interpretation suggests orientation in the modern age as the goddess and feminine power returns to the West (p. 14-15). All of this information suggests the importance of a Dark Goddess event and what the content of those events would be.

The World Today and the Inner World

The world today, some would say, makes it difficult for a person to drop into their own inner world, which is the place where the Dark Goddess Journey takes place. This further underscores the importance of creating sacred space (like a women's group) where inner reflection is possible—because it is so needed in today's unsettled and fast-paced times. Another reflection on the difference between this feminine initiation and a patriarchal mode of being comes from German-Jewish art historian Aby Warburg, "In the form of technological mastery over the natural resources on which human survival persists, modernity radically transforms the conditions of artistic and cultural reflexes, destroying the distance that shapes what Warburg called *Denkraum:* the 'space for devotion and reflection' (Pollock, & Turvey-Sauron, 2007, p. 18). "In Warburg's terms, it is perhaps a necessary condition for any art at all which arises in that space for devotion and reflection that sense of human/other relations, dependency and mystery, that has taken so many forms over the millennia of conscious, socialized human existence" (p. 18). The group which could be held at the Full Circle group or elsewhere in the future could be a space for conscious shared reflection, in which women can share with others. This space beyond the regular world can be helpful to tend to the inner world for moving through a Dark Goddess Journey.

The Feminine and Interconnection

Another theme that reoccurs in interpretations of the Dark Goddess mythology that could inform future meetings at Full Circle or another group, is a sense of shared connection between the Self and others. This interconnection includes both the self and the outside world rather than pulling them apart as discrete and separate. The hero makes himself separate, journeying away from mother to win his victories in the world so he can return as a distinct self. The themes of Mother and Son are important because when a child is created he is originally united with the mother, and thus not separate. The birthing process requires some separation, but less than that required in the Hero's Journey. A feminine journey is one that maintains connections socially. This can be seen as an analogy for the initiation into spiritual states of being connected to all that is, or spiritual surrender and interconnection with the divine and Universe. Pollock (2007) describes another way of being beyond seeing people as separate and quotes Ettinger, "Here along the metamorphic borderlines, the other and I share connections that when fading by ways of transformation are leaving traces in both" (p. 44). This is an inherent interconnection rather than a goal to separate and individuate such as in the Hero's Journey. It is possible to be a separate self and also be interconnected. This is a big theme for women because of the encouragement they receive in our society to be relational, while also expected to be independent because the dominant culture in America rewards independent achievement. Working together in a group to look into one's own life experience and share that would be beneficial to help women balance self and other.

This passage from a space of duality—which either connects or separates people from each other—and into a space of interconnection, is part of the feminine initiation and transcendence of limitations. The ego is forced to reconcile with a new way of thinking and being—which may require a level of death and rebirth, so that life can be seen with new eyes. Even if all seems identical from an external point of view, an awakening has occurred inside. In this space one can let go of wounds, draw healthy boundaries, and yet see how everything in self and life is allowed, perfect, and connected in its own way. Group work with the feminine divine ultimately leads to reconnection with anything that seems opposite—including power, shadow, the world, wounds, and the masculine in a healthy way.

Personal Context

In writing this paper I, as the author, must acknowledge my perspective and how it affects my presentation. My concept of the divine, as well as the world of shadow work is colored by my own lens. This section will describe my own perspective and illuminate how I may be open or not open to information that would further the cause of facilitating a Dark Goddess journey group. First, my attraction to the Goddess is natural for me considering my history: I did not have a strong mother figure growing up, so I was drawn to feminine images of the divine. Second, I had negative mothering experiences from my stepmother, which has made it difficult for me to feel empowered as a young adult. Staying safe became very important, so I was especially cautious about taking up space, being noticed, or being vulnerable—much of my true personality ended up veiled in the shadow to protect myself. I also became aware in late high school and college that there were aspects of myself that either let people walk all over me or were sabotaging my attempts to receive more in life. In trying to overcome this, I found that this pattern repeated because I had earlier put parts of my power into the shadow, partially to stay safe from my stepmother, but also to rebel and fight her by being nothing like her at all. I needed to reclaim some of that darkness to find more balance. There were things I needed to reexamine and remove from the shadow—to add to my toolbox even if they seemed mean or not nice, or something like my stepmother that I resisted a great deal. This process of recovering parts of myself was uncomfortable and reminds me of those Goddess myths. My early twenties were a time of exploration—exploring my negative patterns, therapy, journaling, and creativity that occurred at the same time I reacquainted myself with the Goddess. Taboo areas like money, sexuality and my curiosity around witchcraft became a part of this journey. Much of this journey I carried through alone until I found spiritual women's groups like Full Circle and online. Only then did I recognize the healing power of sharing authentically with others in a sacred space dedicated to the divine, including where the Goddess is honored and respected. I want to give others that gift of transformation that the Goddess and opening to connection gave to me. These aspects of my experience make me want to explore themes related to the Dark Goddess in sacred community and help others to contemplate it more deeply.

Because I found my early childhood events to be disempowering, I resonate with the myths of the Dark Goddess that involve engaging with intense material and transforming it. I've also been drawn to female empowerment from a young age, and originally studied international relations and political science as an undergraduate to help women and thus all of humanity as a diplomat. I had read studies as a teen about how helping mothers helps the children and the husband. I never imagined my path would eventually lead to the healing work, coaching and writing that I do professionally now—or the spiritual work I feel called to do—but I can see the seeds of that early fascination with women's empowerment on a global scale. I enjoy discussion with the Full Circle members around feminism and how it seems connected to the spiritual earth-based movement as well.

Full Circle members and I have also discussed how an unfortunate event can be reinterpreted to be empowering. Discussion from Full Circle helped me to understand how the tale of Persephone could be empowering rather than depressing. In many ways that is similar to life: Through writing, contemplation, meditation and sharing with positive women, I can come to reinterpret my personal myths and see my personal power radiating through. I can reinterpret my mother's death that profoundly affected me in a sad way, as an important milestone in my life that made me who I am—and for that I am grateful. My strength to love my stepmother even though she emotionally hurt me shows how amazing my ability to love is—and not view it as a weakness.

No one can feel their power fully if they are still in the underworld journey of feeling unfairly victimized. I feel strongly now that I have seen the light and that I'm here to help others out, too. To feel powerful is the opposite of feeling like a victim to a force—which for other women might include institutional oppression, a family structure, loss or something else. We all deserve that. Empowered, together we can make a better world.

As I move forward into my thirties, I'm a changed version of my earlier self. Even coming out of an academic Master's program in a Jesuit environment like Loyola, I feel a sense of freedom to discuss other topics in my spiritual work. I would like to be more open about how sensual and sacred sexuality has influenced my journey and contributed to my ascent from the shadow.

Today many women are discussing their sexual traumas, shames, and anger at the masculine, the hierarchy, money systems, and so on. There is healing to be done in the area of sexuality, and although it felt rather "taboo" for me to discuss in depth in an academic environment, I look forward to including sexuality in women's discussion groups. I know this topic can help women to tap into sacred sexual and sensual power in their voyage down into and out of their personal underworld. I do believe that in a previous time some of us women were sexual healers, or conduits for fertility rites and expressions of love in divine partnership, and I've realized that I believe I have been a sacred sexual priestess in another life. I think that this energy can also be raised alone, and in the modern day we find new ways to work with it to serve us safely. These are joyful shadow areas to be healed both culturally and individually for many women. Perhaps this will be a part of live events, private work, writing, or teaching for me in the future.

My ideas for a future Dark Goddess event, the content of exercises, and so forth is colored by my experience. Recently, I have channeled information from Dark Goddess work that my process through the underworld includes four stages, at least. My process begins with a period of grappling with loss feelings, a rumbling with power issues or definitions, a creative period that helps me get clear, and finally a reconnection to soul outside or inside of myself that is truly beautiful, and then the cycle begins again. This will likely inform my teaching and facilitation style, but I endeavor to help others to find out more about their unique process.

The Dark Goddess as an archetype is a rich source of themes that would benefit many women. Mythology, scriptures, psychology and feminist theory illuminate how this theme connects to and empowers women to live their best lives. Through the exploration of difficult emotions, oppression, limitations and ways that they have given away their power, women can tap into a source of greater light and power held within the archetype of the Dark Goddess.

References:

Babcock, L., & Laschever, S. (2007). *Women Don't Ask: The High Cost of Avoiding Negotiation--and Positive Strategies for Change.* New York, NY: Bantam.

Campbell, J. (2008). *The Hero with a Thousand Faces.* Novato, CA: New World Library.

Craighead, W. E., & Nemeroff, C. B. (Eds.). (2004). *The Concise Corsini Encyclopedia of Psychology and Behavioral Science.* Hoboken, NJ: John Wiley & Sons.

Cunningham, S. (2015). *Wicca: A guide for the solitary practitioner.* Woodbury, MN: Llewellyn Publications.

Ford, D. (1998). *Dark Side of the Light Chasers: Reclaiming Your Power, Creativity, Brilliance and Dreams.* New York, NY: G P Putnam's Sons.

Foucault, M. (1995). *Discipline and Punish: The Birth of the Prison* (2nd ed.) (A. Sheridan, Trans.). New York, NY: Vintage Books.
Frye, M. (1983). *The Politics of reality: Essays in feminist theory.* Freedom, CA: The Crossing Press.

Gadon, E. (1989). *The Once and Future Goddess: A Sweeping Visual Chronicle of the Sacred Female and Her Reemergence in the Cultural Mythology of Our Time.* San Francisco, CA: HarperOne.

Grabe, S. (2010). *Feminism and women's rights worldwide* (Vol. 3) (M. A. Paludi, Ed.). Santa Barbara (Calif.): Praeger.

Perera, S. B. (1989). *Descent to the goddess: A way of initiation for women.* Toronto: Inner City Books.

Pollock, G., & Turvey-Sauron, V. (Eds.). (2007). *The Sacred and the Feminine: Imagination and Sexual Difference* (New Encounters: Arts, Cultures, Concepts). New York, NY: I.B.Tauris.

Reis, E. (1999). *Damned women: Sinners and witches in Puritan New England.* Ithaca: Cornell University Press.

For Inanna, Who Cannot be Contained by a Grave
Amanda Lee Morris

Inanna, who is also called Ishtar and Astarte
    Who has endless names unknown or unspoken
Who is also called Queen of Heaven and Queen of the Earth
    and Mistress of All the Universe

As the evening and morning star
You shine on us as the sun is setting
Your light carries us through the night and through our darkest hours
You shine on us when the sun is rising
Your light adding to that of the day and to our brightest hours.

With a crown of stars, of gemstones, of a million leaves, petals, and horns
    You rule over all the realms
And it is an honor, indeed, to be ruled by you.

You decorate your breast with stars
    with lapis, agate, and pearls the color of the brightest rainbows
But it is you who give jewels and the cosmos their luster
For even naked and alone and hung up on a meat hook in the underworld
You are still the most treasured beauty of both heaven and of earth.

For ages unto ages, poets have given their words to you
But one poem is not enough
Nine prayers are not enough
50,000 words are not enough

Seven epics are not enough
To contain your glory

And so shine on, glorious Queen, mistress, and Goddess.
May your brightness never fade
And may we always appreciate the bright blessings and dark lessons you bestow upon us all.

Flight
Patricia Ballentine

Making Our Stand

Molly Remer

> "You may not remember,
> but let me tell you this,
> someone in some future time
> will think of us."
> —*Sappho*

I put on my boots and jeans, grab my priestess robe, pack a basket of ritual supplies, and meet four close friends in a nearby cave. We feel a little nervous about holding ritual on unfamiliar land, but we decide to push our boundaries and do it anyway. *The land needs us*, says my friend. *The other people who come here are meth-heads and vandals.*

We take our drums and climb to the top of the cave, singing as we find our way up the steep hillside. On top, looking out across the country, we sing: *cauldron of changes, feather on the bone, arc of eternity, ring around the stone*. We laugh and practice some more songs, some hearty, some tentative and new. We tie up small bundles of our symbolic burdens with stones and let them down over the edge using hand-spun wool yarn until the yarn releases, taking our burdens with them. Suddenly, we hear the sound of tires on the gravel. Slamming doors. The sound of loud men's voices. The smell of cigarette smoke. A ripple of uncertainty passes through us. We are once again tentative and we feel a current of unease. *What should we do?* we whisper to one another. The voices draw nearer, there are calls and hoots. My friend looks at me and says: *This is where we make our stand.* We hold hands in a line at the edge of the cave roof, gazing out into the horizon. A hawk wheels overhead. We sing. The approaching voices quiet. We sing louder.

> *I am a strong woman, I am a story woman, I am a healer, my soul will never die.*

We project our voices and yell: *We are the witches, back from the dead!*

The voices stop. We wait. We hear doors slamming. The sound of tires on gravel. We are alone once more.

We descend into the cave singing a song composed on the spot: *Deeper, deeper. We're going deeper. Deeper, deeper. Deeper still.*

We strike a pose based on the carvings described in the classic book, *When the Drummers were Women*. Archaeologists described carvings of priestesses carrying drums as, "women carrying cakes to their husbands."

We shout: *"We're not carrying cakes!"*

I stand on a rock in the center of the cave and sing: *She's been waiting, waiting, she's been waiting so long, she's been waiting for her children to remember to return.* My friends join the song and we move deep into the darkness where we face the "birth canal" at the back of the cave, listening to the small stream within trickle, laugh, and bubble as it emerges from the dark spaces deep within the heart of the earth. We begin to sing:

> *Ancient mother we hear you calling. Ancient mother, we hear your song. Ancient mother, we hear your laughter...*

Just as we sing the words, *ancient mother, we taste your tears,* droplets of cave water fall on our faces, splashing our eyelids.

It might seem simple on the surface, but gathering the women and calling the circle is a radical and subversive act.

A revolutionary act. In my work with women's circles and priestessing, I am repeatedly reminded that gathering with other women in a circle for ritual and ceremony is deeply important even though it might just *look* like people having fun or even being frivolous, it is actually a microcosm of the macrocosm—a miniature version of the world we'd like to see and that we want to make possible.

In the book, *Casting the Circle,* Diane Stein observes that women's rituals, "...create a microcosm, a 'little universe' within which women try out what they want the macrocosm, the 'big universe' or real world to be. Within the safety and protected space of the cast circle, women create their idea of what the world would be like to live in under matriarchal/Goddess women's values... The woman who in the safety of the cast circle designs the world as she would like it to be takes that memory of creation and success out into daily life... By empowering women through the microcosm of the ritual's cast circle, change becomes possible in the macrocosm real world" (p. 2-3).

It starts with these private ritual and personal connections and then, as Stein explains, "A group of five such like-minded women will then set out to clean up a stream bed or park in their neighborhood; a group of twenty-five will join a protest march for women's reproductive rights; a group of a hundred will set up a peace encampment. The numbers grow, the women elect officials to government who speak for their values and concerns. Apartheid crumbles and totalitarian regimes in Eastern Europe end, disarmament begins, and laws to control polluters are enforced. Homes, foods, and jobs are opened to the world's homeless, and often begins in the microcosm of the Women's Spirituality ritual circle" (p. 3).

> *Circle round*
> *circle round and celebrate*
> *circle round and sing*

circle round and share stories
circle round and reach out a hand
circle

no beginning
no end...

In my college classes, I often told my students that in working with people, we need to learn to think in circles, rather than in lines. Circles are strong. Circles are steady. Circles hold the space, circles make a place for others. Circles can expand or contract as needed. Circles can be permeable and yet have a strong boundary. Linked arms in a circle can keep things out and show solidarity. Linked energy in a circle can transform the ordinary into sacred space. Hands at each other's backs, facing each other, eye level. Working together in a circle for a ritual, change is birthed, friendships are strengthened, and love is visible.

As I read news stories about the incredible, unimaginable violence and brutality experienced by women around the world, it can be easy to become depressed and discouraged and to feel like our efforts are hopeless. I return to a conversation I had with a friend before one of our women's circle gatherings... Does it really *matter* that we do this or is it a self-indulgence? After some debate, we concluded that it *does* matter. That actively creating the kind of woman-affirming world we want to live in is a worthy, and even holy, task. I've successfully created a women's subculture for myself and those around me that comes from an ecofeminist worldview. However, is that *actually creating change*? Or, is that just operating within the confines of a damaging, restrictive, and oppressive social and political structure?

Some time ago, I facilitated a *Cakes for the Queen of Heaven* series and I made a mistake when I was talking saying, "*in the land that I come from...*" rather than saying, "in my perspective" or "in my worldview." This is now a joke amongst my circle of friends, we will say, "in my land... that isn't what happens," or "let me tell you what it is like in my land." I have to feel like that *does* make a difference. If we can share "our land" with others, isn't change possible? Doesn't "our land" have inherent value that is worth promoting, protecting, and populating?

> *"Feminist ritual practice is currently the most important model for symbolic and therefore, psychic and spiritual change in women. Certainly ritual is an idealized microcosmic experience, but it may be an endurably important means of invoking a new order of things in the macrocosm. At the very least, it has been a useful mode for envisioning what a different world for women might 'feel' like."* -Kay Turner (*The Politics of Women's Spirituality*)

The women have gathered in a large open living room, under high ceilings and banisters draped with goddess tapestries, and their faces are turned toward me, waiting expectantly. We are here for an overnight Red Tent Retreat and we are preparing to go on a pilgrimage. I tell them a synopsis version of Inanna's descent into the underworld, her passage through seven gates and the requirement that at each gate she lie down something of herself, to give up or sacrifice something she holds dear, until she arrives naked and shaking in the depths of the underworld, with nothing left to offer, but her life.

In our own lives, I explain, we face Inanna's descents of our own. They may be as difficult as the death of an adult child, the loss of a baby, the diagnosis of significant illness, or a destroyed relationship. They may be as beautiful and yet soul-wrenchingly difficult as journeying through childbirth and walking through the underworld of postpartum with our newborns. They may be as seemingly everyday as returning to school after a long absence. There is value in seeing our lives through this mythopoetic lens. When we story our realities, we find a connection to the experiences and courage of others, we find a pattern of our own lives, and we find a strength of purpose to go on.

My parents have a lodge close to a river. On the property, there are two springs, one smaller and easily accessible, the other issuing forth three million gallons of water a day, but farther away, along a narrow trail through the woods and along the river bank. Today, we will pilgrimage to the second spring to collect some sacred water for our ritual. I invite the gathered women to join me on this pilgrimage, explaining that in some way, they will pass through gates of their lives as they walk, that they will likely have to lay down something, and that, I promise, they will learn something about themselves. While there is power in guided meditations and visualizations that take you to sacred springs, I say, there is nothing like actually *doing it*. Rather than imagine we are walking through the green woods, along the river bank, listening to bird song, and the sound of flowing water, we will actually be doing those things, *together*.

Seven women accept my invitation and we set off together, picking our way first through rocks and then through muddy puddles and slippery grasses. I am a little nervous as we proceed. What if I have promised a magical story, a lesson, an adventure that cannot actually be delivered? As we walk the increasingly narrow trail, bordered by rock on one side and the river on the other, we do indeed pass through several gates, one created by a fallen tree trunk bridging across the trail, another created by a very small spring that emerges from a small cave and flows across mossy rocks to join the creek created by the large spring. The rocks are slippery and navigation is difficult, most of us emerge from this "gate" with wet feet and shoes.

We reach the large spring at last, muddy feet, wet shoes, sweaty faces, bug bitten thighs. I climb down the steep hillside to where I can reach the water, filling the two jars I have brought with me for this purpose. Before we do so, we sing in gratitude for that which we are receiving. I hold the jars aloft and say, *we return, bearing this sacred water for our people!* A few feet away, one of my friends, a comfortably large woman with a goddess of Willendorf style build, asks if I mind if she takes a dip. She slips out of her caftan and stands for a moment on the rock, unapologetically naked under the blue sky. She slips easily beneath the water, fully immersed, and then emerges, icy water rippling down her full form. I love that one of us has in fact, become fully naked and unadorned in the "underworld" of our journey together.

On our return path, the larger group moves quickly ahead. I am carrying both jars of water and walk slowly with the two friends who have given up their shoes on our descent and who have to walk carefully across the uneven ground. We reach a bend in the creek and a point in the trail at which we must boost ourselves up by an exposed root. My shoeless friend reaches her hand to the root and as she does so a fallen log dislodges and rolls down the hillside at her, bringing a startlingly loud shower of dirt and small rocks with it. A friend further ahead on the trail turns back, reaching her hand down for our water jugs, so that I can reach my hand down to our other friend. She tucks the jars of water into her shoulder bag and then leans back over towards us to help. Suddenly, there is a thud, a rolling sound, and a splash. One jar of sacred water has rolled from her bag, down the bank and landed with a splash in the creek, where it is immediately whisked away by the current. *Our sacred water!* I cry. *Oh, Inanna...* calls one friend, with a small smile and a wry shake of her head. The woman who dropped it immediately sets off along the trail, running along the narrow path, the bobbing jar still in her sights as it navigates the curves of water.

The rest of us continue to walk. We lose sight of our friend. We reach the point of the creek in which we think she would have gone through the woods to try to retrieve the water and she isn't there. We call her name and she doesn't answer. We feel a small edge of concern. Where did she go? I find myself musing about what lesson can be found in pilgrimaging to acquire something and then losing it and returning empty-handed. There is a mythopoetic understanding to be found within that as well, I'm certain, though less exciting than returning with the gift we have promised to share with our people!

Then, ahead of us on the trail, after the cliffside, and where the path opens back up into grassy bottomland again, we finally see our friend. She is immersed to her waist in the icy water and in her hands, held to the sky, she holds our jar of sacred water.

We are full of excitement as we return, chattering about the rescue of the water, her daring plunge into the current to retrieve it, and the physical reality of our own shero's journey of descent and return. *I'm totally writing about this!* I say, *do I have your permission?* She laughs and says, *I love how this story has become about me rescuing the water instead losing it in the first place!*

We return to the rest of our friends at the lodge, where they have been dyeing prayer flags with indigo. Before we go in, my barefoot friend touches my arm and asks to take a selfie with me. My hand goes to my sweaty, disheveled hair, I know my face is red from heat. *I want it just like this*, she says, *to remember this wildness*.

Inside, we share our sacred water with the others. We dip it into small spray bottles which also contain small gemstones and essential oils with names like Serenity and Balance. This water ends up traveling to Germany with one friend, who uses it to center herself while traveling. It blesses a mother and new baby at a baby blessing ceremony. I use it as a sacred space spray to clear my workspace before settling down at my computer. It is used in the footbath for a maiden at her first moon ritual.

This water is imbued with our collective magic, the reminder that what is lost, can be found again, plucked from the current and into the story of our lives.

Originally published in SageWoman Magazine.

My Name is Inanna
Arna Baartz

Illustration from *My Name is Inanna*.

I Can Hear Her

Annie Finch

A young goddess, full of love, fresh with the touch of a husband, carrying power and rich with anger, strength, urgency, understanding,

follows the direction her ear has led her, down to the place where the underworld glistens.

At each door she removes a jewel, a belt, a ceremonial robe.

At each door, she is less and more. She bows down through the seventh door.

The young goddess is dead, and waiting. The young goddess is dead.

A goddess goes down, and I can see her. She needs to go, decides to go.

A goddess goes down, and I can hear her.

First published in Eve by Annie Finch (Story Line Press, 1997).

The Song of Inanna
Liliana Kleiner

Ten years ago, in Jerusalem of 2007, I published my first art book, "The Song of Lilith." The mythological Lilith revealed herself to me in a dream while I was living and working in Montreal in 1990's and immersed in dream work. In a numinous dream, 'Shulamit,' an older, dark woman, walking in a forest, gave me a book with a black cover and on it was printed in big red letters the name: "LILITH." I had no idea who she was other than relating her to my own name—Lili, short for Liliana, or 'Lilita', as my mother used to call me as a child. For many years I researched the archetypal mythological character of Lilith, giving her life and expression through paintings, prints, poems and performances, such as "Psyche and Lilith" (Montreal 1990) and films, "Lilith and the Tree" (16mm, 1993). The work reached its culmination in the creation of a handmade artist book—"The Song of Lilith." This original handmade book was reproduced and published in Jerusalem 2007, about 17 years after my initial dream of Lilith. A week later, as I was walking downtown Vancouver with my new book tucked under my arm, I run into a man selling second-hand stuff on the side walk. My eyes landed on a book called: "INANNA—from the Myth of Ancient Sumer," a collection of her stories by Kim Echlin.

As with Lilith's sudden appearance in my life years before, Inanna's myth was unknown to me, but as I browsed through the first pages of the book, a myth from about 6,000 years ago, I felt immediately drawn into Inanna's world; she was calling me to discover and recover her stories as the 'mother' of Lilith, her ancestor in middle eastern mythology. I quickly learned that Inanna, Queen and Goddess of ancient Sumer, Iraq of today, is the oldest recorded myth in Western civilization, carved on clay tablets with the first known alphabet in the West. This rich legacy, recorded thousands of years before the Bible, the Koran and the

Greek myths, has been mostly erased, forgotten or rejected by modern historical records.

I started my love affair with Inanna in the fall of 2008. For the next few years, magical events kept guiding me while I was researching her origins through books, resources and visits to museums around the world. Once, when I was in Berlin participating in an art show called 'Jewish Women Artists dispersed around the world,' I visited the Pergamon Museum and was amazed to come face to face with the gates of the ancient temple of Inanna from Sumer! They were beautifully preserved in all their magnificence and on display in a museum in Berlin, of all places.

Inanna's stories were written at the time when the Goddess religions were still very present but already beginning to lose their hold on the general population. The Goddess and Great Mother were challenged by God, the Father. Societies were changing from a nomadic lifestyle into an agricultural one and the practice of ownership was growing. The Goddess religions and the Nomadic life were mostly in harmony with Nature, but agricultural development demanded control over wild Mother Nature. Simultaneously, on an individual level, the unconscious participation with the Great Mother (the feminine 'par excellence') was challenged by a new developing Ego consciousness, based on 'thinking,' the masculine principle of 'intellect.' Humans were creating the alphabet for writing and recording. Nomads recorded by heart and traveled light, whereas farmers and owners needed written records and rules 'set in stone' (like the 'Ten Commandments'). The evolution of consciousness required that we separate from the Great Mother and become aware of ourselves as separated from Nature and from Mother, individually and collectively, separate from both the personal and the universal Mother. In accordance, the Biblical creation story tells that the "Word" created the world and that man 'gave birth' to woman, she came second, out of his rib.

It seems that the evolution of Consciousness in humans evolved by sacrificing the feminine, by having the masculine take over 'The Mother.' As a result the Goddess Feminine Spirit in its Totality — the living spirit in all Matter—has been repressed and devalued for the last 5000 years of patriarchy. Seen matter as soulless, as 'just material,' and thinking God is disconnected from Mother Earth and not in Her, in her essence, has turned sacred matter into unrestrained 'materialism', with capitalism as the new religion and consumerism its sacred practice.

Accordingly, the 'religion' of Science and technology, based on 'the pure and objective intellect,' a known masculine power, became more precious than ethics, philosophy, the 'social sciences' and the arts, the realms of the feminine, associated with depth of feeling and aesthetics, the sense beauty. In this new world, undoubtedly Man becomes more valuable than woman and Men more important than Mother Nature. Emotionally, the opposition of matter and spirit cuts us off from both Mother Nature and from our own original individual nature, giving birth to an ever-present sense of longing—a visceral craving to reunite body and soul and end the devastating feeling of alienation typical of modern life.

This alienation from our roots on the Earth and from our own depth of feeling, makes us search for meaning and wholeness in all the 'wrong places,' such as addictions, worshiping money and fame, and being constantly busy. The masculine archetype has been predominant for thousands of years, devaluing and subjugating the feminine to its power and control. The next evolution of consciousness depends on our ability to face and integrate these opposites in ourselves, embracing the tension between the masculine and feminine principles with an understanding that their imbalance lies at the root of sexism, racism and classism, and most important today, at the root of our environmental management and ecology.

Inanna's myth seems to come from a group psyche that felt and saw this tension of opposites and responded with a vision of integration. An awareness that saw how the masculine was beginning to overpower the feminine and called for unity and wholeness on a personal and collective way. Since we live according to the story we buy into, we require myths to awaken our spirits into higher planes. The Grail was likely the last living myth of Europe that called for the consciousness of the Bleeding Heart, the revival of the feminine, and for compassion as a 'religious' way of life, a vision that is carried on today by the Dali Lama. We need new myths where the metaphors for spirit and courage are not Male gods in the sky, but feminine wisdom and Earth values. Such was the Mexican myth of the Virgin of Guadalupe, the Black Madonna patron of the Mexican Revolution. This modern myth dared to redeem the spiritual feminine and its native ancient roots. Guadalupe looks just like any 'mamacita,' a native Earthy-woman, very unlike the white Virgin Maria, mother of Jesus, or her opposite, Maria Magdalene, the prostitute. The myth of Guadalupe attempted to restore the feminine Spirit down on Earth, however Guadalupe got trapped in the realms of the Fathers of the Church, who adopted her in order to control her powerful independent power on her people.

The Sacred feminine is still very much alive in Wild Nature where the 'hand of man' had not yet tamed or raped mother Earth for its use and abuse. When we experience Nature in its wild force and beauty, we are obliged to bow down to it in awe and feel in all modesty that we are just a tiny part of this magnificent universe. This encounter, besides waking us to our true original roots, can bring our inflated ego down to Earth, an experience that is most humbling, healthy and necessary for growth. Away from Wild Nature, in our modern urban lives, the Sacred Feminine can reach us through love and the imagination, the arts, dreams, myths and stories, touching our souls and awakening the uncontaminated life forces, the real true forces of rebirth living in our unconscious.

History shows again and again that our 'normal' ego mind-consciousness is not enough to manifest critical lasting changes in humanity. Thinking alone is not sufficient—we need the powers of the imagination, of the heart and spirit.

Inanna's stories have the potential to awaken in ourselves new forces. Her ancient wisdom is likely to revive feelings and insights that are buried deep in our collective unconscious for generations, and even evoke the self-knowledge needed for a lasting change from the roots up. Inanna's message is not about reversing back patriarchy into matriarchy, making strong women and weak men as typical of the submission-domination paradigm. Hers is the 'middle road,' the path of individual integration and participation with all life on Earth. Like a modern "Grail," Inanna brings a message of healing to our wounded hearts, opening new doors of perceptions into a consciousness of wholeness by embracing the rejected Sacred Feminine in its Totality.

The writer, like the artist, composer, and inventor, all have a fundamental need to discover and create something new and whole, to express the beauty and harmony that is clearly found and seen in nature, a new psyche leading to new orders. Inanna's stories come from such a creative impulse, they are the creation of a psyche in search for Unity, the unity of the three worlds that have been separated, the re-union of Heaven, Earth and the Underworld; spirit, matter and psyche.

Excerpt from Liliana Kleiner's book, 'The SONG of INANNA,' which recounts the original ancient myth of the Goddess Inanna, from 6000 years ago in Sumer, and presents a Psychosocial, Jungian Feminist analysis relevant to our modern times.

Produced in Jerusalem, November 2017, by Jerusalem Fine Art Prints Ltd., the book includes a collection of Liliana's original artwork inspired by Inanna's eye-opening stories.

"The Song of Inanna" by Liliana Kleiner.

To Dance Her Seven Veils
Nuit Moore

As a priestess of the ancient Sumerian Goddess Inanna, I serve Her and celebrate Her mysteries in various ways. One of these ways is through the vehicle of transcendent dance. Transcendent and ecstatic dance is one of the most ancient ritual components of spiritual practice and worship.

I combine tribal modern dance with the foundation of transcendent ecstatic dance to create a fusion that expresses the sacred symbolism of the Mysteries of Inanna, as well as the other Goddesses my temple serves. In fact, it was said that the secrets of the mystery religions of ancient times could be found in the language of the associated ceremonial dances of the particular mysteries; the ancient Greek rhetorician Lucian stated in his writings on dance that one "cannot find single ancient mystery in which there is not dancing... of those who reveal the mysteries that they 'dance them out.'"

Another area in which I am able to combine the sacred aspects of dance with my spiritual practice is in the Mysteries of the Veil, which I have studied extensively. The Veil is so rich in mystic symbolism that I will only touch on its relevance within sacred dance and how I incorporate these mysteries in ritual practice and performance. The veil is a very popular implement within Tribal and Orientale belly dance, and has a long association with dance, as well as with the Mysteries of the Goddess. The veil is one of the most ancient and powerful of symbols of the Goddess, representing that which is unseen, hidden, the secret workings of Fate... that which is beyond our mortal ken.

There is a devotional piece I perform as priestess based on one of the most well-known marriages of the veil with dance: the Dance of the Seven Veils. Although there is much speculation on the authenticity of the time and origin of the Dance of the Seven Veils, the correlations between the Dance of the Seven Veils with the Mysteries of Inanna/Ishtar are a strong indication that there is indeed an ancient origin.

The Dance of the Seven Veils was first mentioned in the play 'Salome' by Oscar Wilde. Salome's dance has been recorded in ancient literature, but Wilde's work is the first known to mention her removing seven veils. I believe that the Biblical story of Salome is connected of the Descent of Inanna, and it would not be surprising as the interpretations found in the Bible took much of the powerful symbolism of the Goddess and reduced it down to negative connotation. The Goddess Herself was changed into "Babylon the Great, Mother of Harlots" in Revelation 17:5. The Biblical interpretation of Salome is no kinder, and expresses her as an icon of the dangerous woman ready to use her wiles and charms to bring about the downfall of men (much in the same vein that the Goddess Lilith was reduced to a succubus). As a result, the Dance of the Seven Veils has been much regarded as a lascivious dance, it's only aim to titillate men with the 'dangerous' sexuality associated with Salome. In addition, the sacred female art of belly dance (and women's dancing in general) has been reduced through the ages as well, now commonly viewed as simply entertainment aimed at pleasing men. The Dance of the Seven Veils IS a sensuous dance, but one of sacred female sexuality, NOT one of the Patriarchal profane.

Inanna is a Goddess of fertility, sensuality, sexuality, fecundity and also of death and rebirth. One of Her most important mysteries along with her Holy Marriage to Dumuzi is Her Descent into the Underworld. In various versions the reason for the Descent differs but the overwhelming message is that Inanna/Ishtar must go into the Underworld to meet her dark sister Ereshkigal in order to obtain salvation for Her lover/people/self. For this journey, the Goddess adorns Herself with seven symbols of Her power. On Her journey, She must pause before entering each of the seven gates to the Underworld and show Her submission and sacrifice by removing one of Her seven symbols of power. Once She has removed the last symbol, She finds Herself naked and bereft in the bowels of the Earth. In the several versions known, the Goddess undergoes a ritual death and achieves resurrection on the third day, which we also find in the mythology of Jesus Christ as well as other resurrection deities. When the Goddess achieves resurrection, She ascends from the Underworld, bringing the precious gift of life and renewal to Her lover, Her people, Her land, and Herself. If ancient adherents of the Mysteries of Inanna did indeed "dance them out" as Lucian suggests, a Dance of the Seven Veils would be a sublimely befitting way to express this Mystery. Another potential aspect of the Dance of the Seven Veils is found in the seven chakras, which can also correlate to the Descent of the Goddess into the Underworld. From the highest spiritual energy center found in the Crown Chakra, we can employ energy work through descending down from the Crown, Third Eye, Throat, Heart, Solar Plexus, Sacrum down to the Root Chakra, which is where we find the dense physical energy of the body, our physical foundation. A good way to symbolize the chakras is to obtain a veil in each of the chakral colors of Violet, Indigo, Blue, Green, Yellow, Orange and Red. Again we find the connection to this Goddess, as one of Her adornments is the rainbow necklace. We also find this connection to the Holy Goddess Isis, who is said to have possessed seven stoles, one in each color of the rainbow.

Another dance that I perform while using veils is the Dance of the Red Goddess, using a pair of red silk veil fans. This dance is also in honor of the Scarlet Goddesses (Inanna/Ishtar/Lilith/Astarte) and is very fluid, punctuated with much hip and pelvic shimmies and wide expansive movements. It is a dance that expresses the fierce female power of the Goddess, Her independent sexuality and celebration of Her wildness. The red veil was also worn by the temple priestesses of Inanna/Ishtar in sexual service, the red symbolizing passion and regeneration. To dance with the Red Veil is to embody the sensual fire of the Goddess, to symbolize the fact that all acts of love and pleasure are indeed Her rituals.

I consider it a devotional duty to the Goddess and to Her daughters to reclaim the sacred sensuality and potent power through the Dance of the Seven Veils. I hope to see the idea of transcendent and ecstatic dance in a sacred context as aspects of ritual and spiritual practice expand and grow, for the joy and release and celebration found in sacred dance devoted to the Goddess is a very fierce and fecund force. It has personally proven to be one of the most powerful offerings of my Temple.

Bibliography:

Inanna: Queen of Heaven and Earth, by Diane Wolkstein and Samuel Noah Kramer, Harper and Row Publishers, 1983.

Sacred Woman, Sacred Dance, by Iris J. Stewart, Inner Traditions International, 2000.

The Ruby in the Lotus, by Nuit Moore, Scarlet Serpent Press, 2007.

Inanna's Ascent
Tara Reynolds

There's a Place for God, and It's in the Bedroom
Glenys Livingstone Ph.D.

In the beginning, long before there was a Word, there was only Matrix and the Matrix was all that was. She was with Herself in the beginning. She needed no holy text. She was Con-text. All that came to be had life in her, nothing was separate from this Teeming Abundant Creativity. This Teeming Abundant Creativity was Felt; and the Feeling was Goddess, Mother, Matrix, Gaia.

When eventually the God did arise, he was not separate, he was part of the Teeming Abundant Creativity, at one with the Matrix. He was in relationship with Her – as son, lover, consort. His body too, like Hers, represented the sacred cycle, of birth, death, and rebirth. He moved through the full circle, like the seasons, like the grain of wheat. He was not eternally erect and dominant. His seed was in Con-text, part of the cycle.

Over the millennia, many stories arose that described the relationship of Goddess and God. One from the oral teachings of the Faerie tradition as told by Starhawk:

> *In love, the Horned God, changing form and changing face, ever seeks the Goddess. In this world, the search and the seeking appear in the Wheel of the Year. She is the Great Mother who gives birth to Him as the Divine Child sun at the Winter Solstice. In Spring, He is sower and seed who grows with the growing light, green as the new shoots. She is the Initiatrix who teaches Him the mysteries. He is the young bull; She the nymph, seductress. In Summer, when light is longest, they meet in union, and the strength of their passion sustains the world. But the God's face darkens as the sun grows weaker, until at last, when the grain is cut for harvest, He too sacrifices Himself to Self*

that all may be nourished. She is the reaper, the grave of earth to which all must return. Throughout the long nights and darkening days, He sleeps in her womb; ... (inhabiting the realm of dreams) ... beyond the gates of time and space, night and day. His dark tomb becomes the womb of rebirth, for at Midwinter She again gives birth to Him. The cycle ends and begins again, and the Wheel of the Year turns, on and on.[3]

This story apparently would belong in what Starhawk calls the Sacred Marriage mythic cycle of the late 4th and 3rd millennium B.C.E.; during this mythic cycle the myths celebrated "the presence of immanent power in the human and natural world, in the seasonal rhythms of renewal and withering, in food and in sexuality."[4] The myth of Inanna and Dumuzi is one of the few written records from that era. In this text, with all its celebration of fertility, it is also quite clear that "sexuality is celebrated for its power to give pleasure and renew all the life on earth"[5] for Inanna never actually gets pregnant. Inanna's love for her own being is explicit, and in Dumuzi, male sexuality is identified as a fructifying force, life-sustaining, food itself.[6] There is no hint at all of a link with violence or dominance. The sexual union of Inanna and Dumuzi is a celebration of the creative, dynamic interplay between these two faces of the Great Mystery of Being.

A transition becomes obvious in the myths from the mid 2nd millennium B.C.E.. Starhawk singles out the Epic of Gilgamesh as representive of this change. With Gilgamesh, she says, we move "out of the stories that link us to the great rounds of birth, death, and renewal; into epic, the recounting of the tales of the hero, the war leader, the great man."[7]

---

3   Starhawk, *The Spiral Dance,* p.43. Brackets my addition.
4   Starhawk, *Truth or Dare,* p.43.
5   Starhawk, *Truth or Dare,* p.44.
6   Starhawk, *Truth or Dare,* p.44.
7   Starhawk, *Truth or Dare,* p.49.

In the Epic of Gilgamesh, the story is quite clearly no longer told from the female point of view, she becomes the "other." Sexual union with her is no longer seen as bringing great good to all the land, Her body has become currency, passed between men for payoffs, entrapments and empire building.[8] It is no longer the Goddess (Inanna and her friends) singing of the erotic, where she chooses her bridegroom and rejoices in him.[9] It is the God (the king Gilgamesh) proving ownership and power, as he takes whomever and whenever he wishes.[10] When Gilgamesh returns victorious from battle and Ishtar chooses him as consort, offering him nourishment and abundance, he refuses her and insults her claiming her food to be tainted and rotten.[11] In lieu of the Sacred Marriage, Gilgamesh becomes great mates with Enkidu as they match each other's strength in a battle at the very threshold of the Goddess' temple.[12] The threshold, Inanna's emblem is destroyed in this battle, recording the portentous abandonment of the ancient celebration of love and fertility.[13]

The epic develops the ideology of warfare. Enkidu and Gilgamesh have many bloodletting adventures together, considered to be heroic as they incite each other to fighting bravely.[14] "Inanna had been the source of the earth's life blood, filling the wells, rivers and springs;"[15] but her blood was not shed with a blade, it was poured forth from her cup as part of the life cycle. Initiation rites that included cutting and the shedding of blood were attempts to emulate this magic, to be like the Goddess.[16] The ritual of warfare added to that a synthetic power that could course through the

---

8   Starhawk, *Truth or Dare,* p.50.
9   Starhawk, *Truth or Dare,* p.45.
10 Starhawk, *Truth or Dare,* p.49.
11 Starhawk, *Truth or Dare,* p.56-57.
12 Starhawk, *Truth or Dare,* p.50.
13 Starhawk, *Truth or Dare,* p.51.
14 Starhawk, *Truth or Dare,* p.51.
15 Barbara Walker, *The Woman's Encyclopedia of Myths and Secrets,* p. 429.
16 Barbara Walker, *The Woman's Encyclopedia of Myths and Secrets,* p. 169.

veins: that of the power to take life, and the appearance of being in control of it.[17]

Yet, there are traces still in this mythic cycle, of the older order and dissatisfactions with the new dominion, as the people complain of the king's arrogance and boundless lust, remembering still that he should be "shepherd of the city, wise, comely and resolute."[18] Also at the end of the tale when Gilgamesh has found the plant that grants immortality, it is stolen from him by a serpent, symbol of the Goddess; and Gilgamesh must die. Gilgamesh is not victorious over the Goddess, he can merely refuse her and insult her and attempt to synthesize her power to take it for himself.

It is in the next mythic cycle, that the patriarchal order triumphs over the old gylanic[19] one. Starhawk sees this triumph typified in the Babylonian creation myth "Enuma elish" from the late 2nd millennium B.C.E.. In this myth, the God Marduk actually does battle with the Goddess Taimat, original progenetrix, primal sea. At this stage in our human story, the divine Female has become the enemy, her erotic power dangerous, the serpent of life-generating waters now a monster of evil. Marduk defeats Her, and creates the world out of Her dismembered body:

> *He split her like a shellfish into two parts:*
> *Half of her he set up and ceiled it as sky,*
> *Pulled down the bar and posted guards.*
> *He bade them to allow not her waters to escape.*[20]

---

17 See Riane Eisler, *The Chalice and the Blade*. Harper & Row, San Francisco. 1987.
18 Starhawk, *Truth or Dare,* p.49, quoting from N.K. Sandars, ed. *The Epic of Gilgamesh,* p.62.
19 A term of Riane Eisler's to describe a matristic/partnership model culture, *The Chalice and the Blade*, p.105.
20 Starhawk, *Truth or Dare*, p.63 quoting from James B. Pritchard, *The Ancient Near East Vol.1: An Anthology of Texts and Pictures*, p.35.

The other gods swear allegiance to Marduk as permanent monarch. Obedience to his word becomes all important, indeed obedience is the "primary condition of the relationship between king and subject."[21] The "God" is praised as avenger and lord, "King of Kings and Lord of Lords."[22]

Perhaps the ultimate victory of Marduk is the socially acceptable genital mutilation of the female, the cutting off of the Goddess' sexual experience. He still daily destroys Her knowledge of Herself in this explicit way; and precludes any possibility of ever being called back to the bedroom again. In this mythic cycle, the Goddess' fierceness and rage is what is remembered of Her,[23] not the reasons for it.

In regards to the place of the biblical text in these mythic cycles, Starhawk comments that although the Bible is directly rooted in the mythology of Mesopotamia, the transition to patriarchy took place long before the first of its books were written down in the late 1st millennium B.C.E.[24] I would suggest that the Bible represents a possible 4th mythic cycle, because here the Goddess is barely mentioned.

Gradually the God overtook the Goddess, and the lap upon which he sat and by which he was king, faded in form until it was stylized to silent throne, unrecognizable as his Mother Queen Goddess.[25] And he forgot his relationship to Her. He ruled alone and has continued to do so. She lost Her face and Her voice and became furniture, as He took over the heavens, conquered every symbol, the language, until now the humans can barely imagine that Mistress could have the same dignity as Master, that the "Light of the World" could be Ishtar, that "God" could be Dumuzi.

---

21 Starhawk, *Truth or Dare,* p.63.
22 Starhawk, *Truth or Dare,* p.65.
23 Starhawk, *Truth or Dare,* p.63.
24 Starhawk, *Truth or Dare,* p.65.
25 See Erich Neumann *The Great Mother.* pp 98-100.

Rosemary Radford Reuther has said that "Male monotheism has been so taken for granted in Christian culture that the peculiarity of imaging God solely through one gender has not been recognized."[26] However, she has still called it "God," and Christian cultures don't have a copyright on this "peculiarity" that she both identifies and perpetuates.

The God of this era, no matter what religion, has forgotten his equality with material reality, forgotten the possibility of honour associated with nourishment, comfort and delight. He has forgotten that he too, at his best, could be part of a mere fertility cult; that is, a spirituality concerned with the life cycle, the reproduction of matter—trivial things like that. His body need not be weapon and alienated. He too is life, He too can serve life, if He comes out of His heavens and back to partnership. The God needs to move out of this freeze He is in, in Father mode, like a moon stuck in full, like a crop of wheat that is never harvested. He needs to remember an intimacy, not just with the Goddess—though certainly with Her—but an intimacy with everything He has felt the need to conquer, transcend and overcome. He needs to remember who He is, that he is a myth, a metaphor. He needs a turn in the underworld, for that is the way of all Being.

As long as religious people and atheists alike, persist in the use of the term "God" as exclusive symbol for the Great Mystery of Existence, it is not possible for the male to be truly partner. The term "God" is a verbal wank, a literal dominance. "God" has become so embedded in our speaking, so essential to human expression that most feel left speechless without it. Even "enlightened" ones continue to use the term, and the capitalized male pronoun, and then deny they are anthropomorphizing the Great Unknowable. If "God" has no gender, why does it feel so viscerally different to use "Goddess"? "She" obviously has a gender, yet "He" does not? Is "He" "All"?

---

26 Rosemary Radford Reuther, "Sexism and God-Language," in Plaskow and Christ, *Weaving the Visions*, p.151.

Even feminist theologians use the term and devote their talent to increasing the God's repertoire of metaphor, working hard to prove that he is mother too, to help him appropriate the feminine qualities of his partner.[27] Zeus and Yahweh don't really need the assistance; they were granted "womblike" abilities thousands of years ago. Why is it necessary to illustrate how "feminine" the God is? Why is it necessary to dress Him in drag? So He can do it all? So She can remain silent, unaddressed, part of the furniture?

There is nothing feminist about "God the Mother"—it is just more colonization. If He is let do the "mothering," the Great Mother Herself will remain lost to us. It is She Herself who wants to constellate again, to manifest. She does not want a disguise, to be Goddess the Father, in Him, with Him and through Him. Though we at this stage find it difficult to imagine, the God's ability to nurture and sustain does not depend on his being "maternal." Takeover is unnecessary, he can re-mythologize himself. He has his own cycles, his own nurturant possibility. There are stories and experience he just has to find again.

It gives one pause to realize that the God never did take on menstruation. He skipped that one, tried the synthetic version. Not even a feminist theologian has claimed that "God can menstruate too." The Goddess' blood, the real stuff, became something that was hidden, a mark of shame and powerlessness instead of a mark of creative power. Perhaps until that cycle is again understood as a metaphor for the sacred, and it won't be until the Goddess is addressed, ecumenism across gender lines is not possible. There can be no real dialogue, if one party does not even really exist, Her country not even in the Atlas, Her name not even spoken. Until "Goddess" can be spoken with the same dignity and comprehensiveness as "God," partnership is not possible.

---

27 For example, see Sallie McFague, "God as Mother", in Plaskow and Christ (ed), *Weaving the Visions*, p.139.

I am reminded of a scene in the movie *Schindler's List*,[28] where the Nazi officer Goeth is confronted with his attraction to his Jewish housekeeper Helen. Spielberg treats it as more than lust, as a temptation to actually love her. He juxtaposes Goeth's reaching out to touch Helen with images of a woman stroking Schindler. Goeth then gets angry as he realizes his impotence to love Helen, blames her for the temptation to this alien feeling of love and relationship, and reverts back to the power he knows. He beats her. Spielberg juxtaposes this beating with Schindler being kissed by the woman relating to him. Was Adam's temptation the same, to actually love Eve? Did he hear for a moment echoes of an older order, wherein Eve offered union, partnership, connection to the cycle of Being, a move back into Con-text? In our mythic cycle will the "God" be able to say "Yes"?

© Glenys Livingstone 1995

This is a slightly edited version of a paper presented by the author at the Religion, Literature and Arts Conference Sydney 1995.

---

28 *Schindler's List* directed by Stephen Spielberg.

References:

Eisler, Riane. *The Chalice and the Blade*. San Fransisco: Harper and Row, 1987.

Neumann, Erich. *The Great Mother.* Princeton: Princeton University Press, 1974.

Plaskow, Judith and Christ, Carol (ed.). *Weaving the Visions*. SF: Harper, 1989.

Pritchard, James B.. *The Ancient Near East Vol.1: An Anthology of Texts and Pictures*. Princeton University Press. 1958.

Sandars, N. K. (ed.). *The Epic of Gilgamesh,* Harmondsworth, Middlesex: Penguin, 1960.

Starhawk. *Truth or Dare*. SF: Harper and Row, 1990.

Walker, Barbara. *The Woman's Encyclopaedia of Myths and Secrets*. San Francisco: Harper and Row, 1983.

Inanna Speaks
Molly Remer

Inanna speaks
she says
*it is time
to step into
the heart of mystery
to set foot
on the path of wild wisdom
to journey to the very depths
of your core.
And once you have descended
deep into the underworld
into the place where
pain and power meet
in the crucible of your life.
Once you are laid bare
stripped raw
and shaking in your bones
you will discover
there is nothing left to fear
there is nothing left to do
there is no one left to please.
You will taste this freedom
in the salt of blood
and the sweetness of wild berries
and then you will turn
naked
unapologetic
and unafraid,
put your feet upon the path
perhaps still unknown,
but unfolding before you
and you will ascend*

through the layers
of that which you no longer need
through the roles that you
no longer inhabit
through the wants that you
no longer fulfill.
You will reclaim your
staff of power
you will accept your
cape of mystery
and you will emerge
from the underworld
with something fierce
blazing in your eyes.
And in the set of your shoulders
and the swirl of your hips
there is something
that can no longer be denied.

You will emerge
Whole.

Spirit Flight
Melissa Stratton Pandina

The Underworld
Talia Segal

I descend into the Underworld wearing nothing but scraps of flesh. I find Ereshkigal and ask Her for help.
"I don't know who I am."
She makes me dig a grave.
This is where you live.
"When can I leave?"
When you are strong enough to leave.
I lay down in the grave and She fills it with Earth.

It's quiet, except when the bugs come. They come and eat the scraps of my flesh until my bones are clean.
Then darkness and quiet.
The memories come next. They stab and whisper insults, but I can't bleed or cry because I'm just bones. They get bored rattling my bones and leave me alone.

I rest in the silent dark. I am not awake and not asleep.
Something changes. A small green light is shining from inside my rib cage.
The change has come because I am no longer afraid. I feel at peace.
I rest and think of my mother. The green light gets stronger, and I recognize my heart chakra being born.
I rest.

My heart buds and flowers. When the petals fall away, the ripe fruit of a new heart is revealed. When the memories come to devour the new flesh, they can't get through my ribcage. They scream in my ears and kick my legs, but my heart beats on. I wait patiently, beatifically.

Alone in the dark, something touches the cold bones of my hand. A tiny seedling has sprouted in my grave. If I had lips, I would smile. With the seedling comes oxygen, and the awareness of two hard little berries near my heart, growing strong and filling with air.

I feel other organs growing. My lungs grow back, slowly. I can't get enough air. My stomach inflates like a balloon, and I feel sick. My eyes open through grit and crust made out of salt from my tears. Being reborn is painful. I cry when the memories come again. Now I can bleed. Now they can hurt me.

I hear my love speaking from a great distance.
"You were broken and forced yourself to mend without healing properly."
"It hurts."
"This time you will heal correctly, but first the scar tissue must be cleaned away."
"But it hurts."
"Just rest. I will protect you."

With renewed strength comes awareness. When the bugs come, I fight them, crushing them with my hands, feet, body. I want to leave. No one can help me. I have to climb out on my own.
I push against the Earth. It rains down into my eyes, my hair, my mouth. I push and pull and spit and curse. I want to leave. I don't belong anymore.

My hand reaches through the hole I made and touches air. I wriggle through the soil and crawl out of the grave at last. My love isn't there. I thought he would be waiting for me. I turn, and Ereshkigal is behind me.
"Where is he?"
I made him leave.
"Why?"
You do not belong here. If he was here when you emerged, you

might have stayed here forever.
I nod, because She is right. I need to get to him. I hear his voice from a great distance, calling me.
I turn to walk up the mountain in the direction I came, but a thought strikes me and I turn back to Her.
"Why are you letting me leave?"
She comes close to me and I see the breadth of Hell in her eyes. *You will be back. But you don't belong here yet.*

I turn and run up the mountain. Rain comes and soaks me, cleans my hair and skin and eyes and skin. My heart pounds, but it is mine. My lungs burn, but they are mine. I reach the top, and take the last step away from the Underworld. My love is waiting for me. I approach him slowly.

"Do you know who I am?"
"Do you know who you are?"
"Yes."
He smiles and offers me his hand.
"You are my great love. Now let's go home."

Rising
Chantal Khoury

Graphite and charcoal on mylar, 2017.

My Shoes
Lennée Reid

Tell me have you walked a mile in my shoes
Were you the one beaten raped?
Were you used?
Were you scared?
How many times were you tested?
How long did you wait
While nobody got arrested?
Could you walk? Could you pee?
Did they let you take a shower?
Was everything all better
When mommy brought you flowers?
So tell me which of these miles you walked
Say exactly where before you begin to talk
Did you roll in a ditch?
Get knocked out hit your head
Did you hear your friend scream?
"Oh my god She's dead?"
Were you the one crying?
Did your heart race
When a loaded gun invaded
Your personal space?
Now did you walk a mile before or after
The shooting ended with thug laughter?
Please here let me take off my heels
You go bury my friends
Tell me how that feels
Speak of the pain and the hurt the despair
You tell me how it feels when nobody cares
Then speak of the faces the places the names
The scenes I just can't seem to erase from my brain
Tell me do you still feel the burn?
Tell me what it is that you have learned?

Did you stop fucking off and leave the party?
To love someone else to be a good mommy
How many years did you spend taking pills?
That doctors said would HELP
Your worries and ills
What was your secret?
How did you survive?
Did you learn to love yourself?
How are YOU alive?
Did you lose the baggage?
Have you recovered?
Do you have wisdom to relate?
Do you care to help others?
Have you been to the mountain top?
What did you see?
Can you describe the sound of emptiness
Filled with eternity?
So please go take a walk in these shoes
I'm done with them now
They're worn all the way through
I have a new spring in my step a new walk
And people seem to listen now when I talk

After the Descent

Tamara Albanna

I have had two times in my life when I made a great descent. From the age of nine months old, leaving my Motherland, Iraq to unknown places due to the tyrannical laws that had taken over the rule of the Goddess, and then at the age of 20, when I left the abusive home of my childhood, and walked into my husband's home.

That first descent was not of my choosing, it was imposed on me. The suffering, the abuse, the breaking of my spirit, being convinced that I was unworthy as a girl child—that my blood was impure, my voice meaningless.

The second descent was made to escape the first. I came up for air, for a brief moment, I was in the light, I was reborn, I was free. This too, was short lived. We all know that even if we change our surroundings, if we haven't reconciled the darkness within, it will follow us everywhere we go—even into paradise.

At 20 years old, I was carrying the emotional baggage of several lifetimes, and only just getting used to the sound of my own voice, the idea of my own agency—that I was a free human being, and this was my birthright.

Like many Iraqi immigrants of the time, we made several stops until we found our "home." From Iraq to Kuwait, then on to the UK, briefly—we finally settled in Canada for four years and lived an (almost) normal existence, until we were dragged out of our environment to go to California. That's when things got very dark. I always vowed I would leave, not matter what it took. So, when the opportunity presented itself, I took it.

My husband and I moved back to Canada, where I found some semblance of happiness, until the illnesses started taking over. My body had held on to so much from my childhood that things all came to head and I was in and out of the hospital. I underwent multiple surgeries and even lost an organ. But, I survived.

Aside from the medical issues, my husband seemed intent on trying to build the perfect spouse. In between the necessary procedures there were others, ones I will not go into—ones that are still too painful to discuss. One in particular had lasting effects on my mothering, and is something I still struggle with. Wounds heal, and scars fade, but the heartache that is implanted is lifelong.

When the one who has promised to love you forever, makes you feel completely unworthy, what are you left with? I still have a hard time with my own reflection, I still do not believe people when they compliment me, because all I wanted was for him to love me, but he couldn't—just like my mother couldn't. I understand now, that this has nothing to do with me, but is in fact their own shadow.

It was the start of my second descent. Don't make any lasting decisions while you are descending—the results can prove devastating.

While pregnant with my first son, I agreed to move to the UAE, as the war in Iraq had just started and we thought since we cannot stop it, we could at least hope to rebuild the motherland. That of course proved to be only a dream, and we should have known, democracy would never come through the barrel of a gun.

I lived in the UAE for over five years, all the while, begging and pleading to go home (Canada). Then another opportunity presented itself, again while I was pregnant, this time with my second son—to move to Austria. Of course I took it; anything to get out of my desert prison.

I thought for sure that after some time in Austria, I would be able to finally go home. Seeing as things in Iraq all went sideways and there was really no hope at that point, I was ready to get on with my life, ready to work and have family around again, ready to be part of a community, have a life. But, again my pleas fell on deaf ears, and at the time of writing this, I have been in Austria for 9 years. Coming up on 15 years living in places I did not want to be, he still would not take me home. My husband chose everything else over me, and I had to accept that. I also had to accept that I had to make my own way.

It is in those 9 years, when Inanna came to me. She came to me at a very pivotal point in my life. And she has not left me since. She handed me the keys to my freedom, to the way out, and most importantly, she told me I was her child. This is why I often refer to her now as my Cosmic Mother.

I am almost 39 years old, I have never had any agency, I have never had a voice, I have never had the chance to build my own life, and decide my own destiny. I also understand that the love I was so desperately seeking, that was so cruelly withheld from me, was something I had carried within me all along. It was not to be found outside of myself at all—it was my very essence.

Today, I see a small glimmer of light. After almost 20 years into this second descent I realize that my time is coming. My descents have been split up into decades, and I understand that now, I understand that I had to do this, I had to go through this, in order to understand what free will was all about.

Descent, Initiation and Return
Heather Mendel

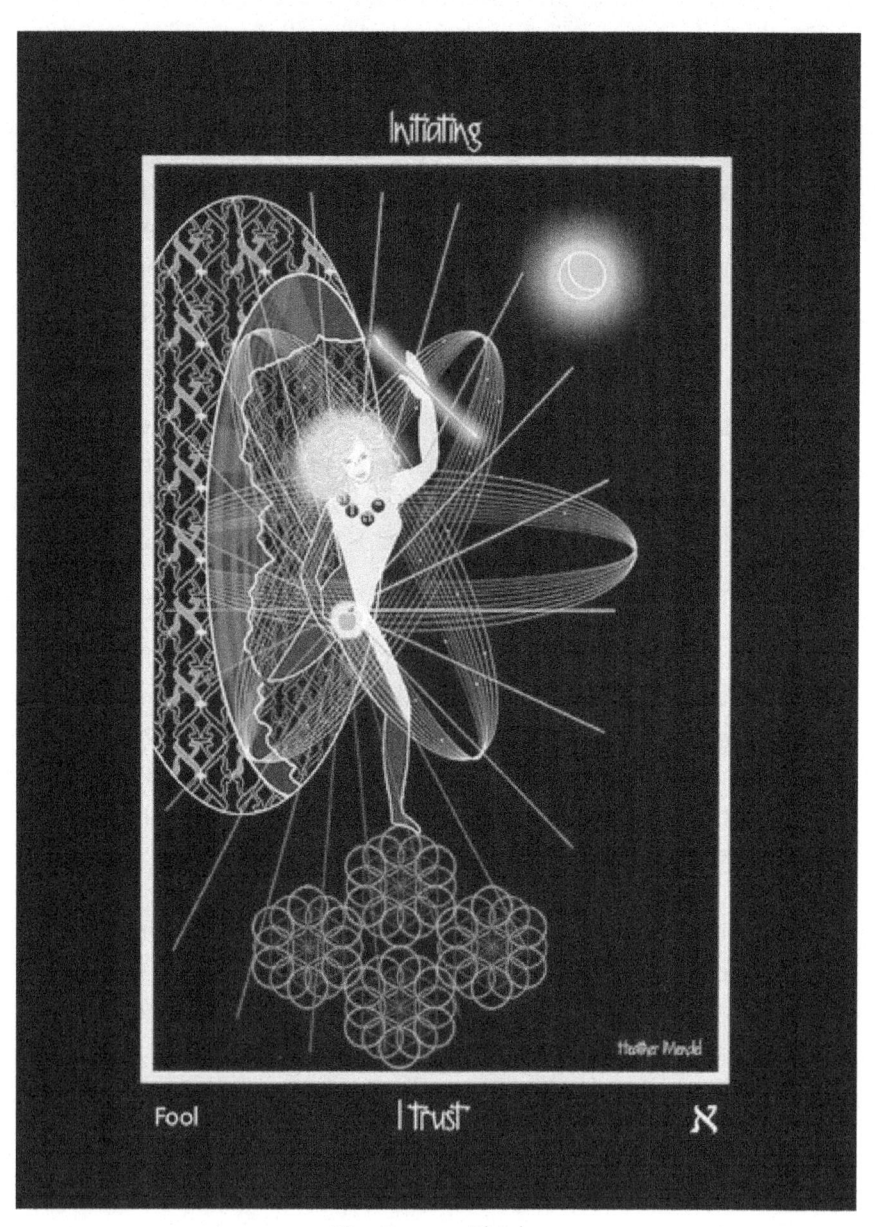

The Syzygy Oracle

Revolving

Wheel I return

Becoming

World   I dance

Myth as a Map to Healing and Wholeness
Heather Mendel

As I reflect on the events of my life, the impact of my personal feminist journey really began in earnest only when I understood the mythic reality of my long, 'dark night of the soul' that had occurred years before. My realization blossomed with my discovery of women's history and spirituality that gave context to my heroine's journey of becoming.

I had been living in South Africa, the country of my birth, during the apartheid era (apartheid is pronounced 'apart-hate' which perfectly explains its ideology). Our social consciousness and conscience was being finely-honed by the horror of living in a system of legalized racism. Being raised in the forties and fifties in a Jewish household, I knew that had I been born in Nazi-controlled Europe around the same time, my life would have been vastly different; the horrors of the Holocaust were just beginning to seep into the awareness of the world community. In South Africa, due to the color of my skin and the privileges I enjoyed, I could have been viewed as part of the oppressors whom I held in such disdain. The polarity of both the oppressor and oppressed was part of my teen consciousness.

In the sixties, I heard about women burning their bras in America but had no idea why. For me, that decade was about doing what was expected—getting a degree in speech and hearing therapy, getting married and having the two children I treasured and welcomed first my son and two years later, my daughter. Over a period of nine years, the joy of family life was marred by the realization that I was in a marriage that was not healthy. My parents, it seemed had been right! At age 19, when I entered this relationship, I realized in hindsight, I was totally unaware of myself, my needs and desires, my strengths and weaknesses.

When divorce was inevitable—and my husband, an emotionally immature man with a vindictive personality streak finally understood that 'saying no' was now an aspect of who I was becoming, and that I was not willing to return to him despite his pleas—he threatened me by stating that I would end up a lonely old woman as he would 'alienate' my son from me. I heard his words but decided these words were just the talk of a wounded angry man who could not get his own way.

In the late seventies, I met and married my soul-mate—a relationship I entered a little more self-aware than the first time. Four years later, our new family—my husband, two children and myself established itself and all seemed so perfect. My 12-year-old son went to visit his father for his summer vacation as planned and never returned. The months-long nightmare of fighting to get him back ended the evening before I was scheduled to appear in court for the custody hearing. My solicitor confirmed that in the trial that would take place the following morning the courts would never remove my custodial rights and would force my son to return to me even if he believed he would prefer to stay with his father.

In the midst of my fear and devastation, I knew that I was not willing to 'cut my son in half' by forcing him to physically be with me while his heart yearned to be elsewhere. With unspeakable heartache and trepidation, feeling his well-being was paramount, I decided not to proceed with the trial, and agreed to allow him to stay with his father. This was my decision, my pain-filled choice. Words cannot portray the depth of despair in making this decision resulting in this separation from my son—in many ways it seemed worse than death, as my first-born child, now no longer part of our family, had rejected me in making his wishes known. Years later, I became aware that my son was raised with the lie that the Courts had removed custody from me and awarded it to his father!

In 1986, four years after this separation, my husband, daughter and I left South Africa for a new life in the United States. Shortly after arriving, I heard Riane Eisler being interviewed as *The Chalice and The Blade* had just been released. As I listened to her speak, a new world vision opened before me. Was it possible that what she was saying about Goddess worshipping cultures was true? Intellectually I queried it but intuitively I had no doubt. Why, I wondered, with the excellent education I had received, had I never heard any of this before?

Her book changed my life. My feminist awakening had begun. Not only did I begin to understand why women had 'burned their bras' in the sixties but that sexism and racism were two sides of the same coin. I started reading everything I could find about prehistory and women's herstory. I was still to learn that what I was doing was a classic example of the heroine's journey after initiation and rebirth—in fact, I only became aware of how perfectly it exemplified Maureen Murdock's work when researching this article.

The heroine's journey, Murdock teaches, is about seeking and healing the wounding of the feminine, both personally and globally, while Campbell's teaching of the masculine hero's journey is about a search for the soul. As women, we separate out from the insidious patriarchal system in which we were raised, and falling into the depths of despair, stripped bare, we experience a spiritual death— in Inanna's story symbolized by her dismemberment prior to her rebirth. Descent for some comes in the form of a yearning for the past, for others as an existentialist crisis at mid-life. For me it was the devastating response to loss and rejection.

In retrospect, I understand there is no way to know how long the departure, let alone the initiation and rebirth will last. In my case it was almost 2 years. I went about my daily activities, numb. I remember seeing the sky was blue, the sun was shining, the flowers bloomed... and it meant absolutely nothing to me. Everything was grey and lifeless. Normally light and color brought me such joy. It was so strange to see others going about their seemingly frivolous lives, unaware that nothing had meaning any longer. In the midst of such depression, it is impossible to recognize that our own view of the world is personal rather than universal.

After reading voraciously about women's spirituality, I attended a workshop with Jean Shinoda Bolen on her book, *Goddesses in Every Woman* and hearing her explanation of the story of Persephone, like a bolt out of the blue, everything fell into place. I realized, not just as a thought, but as an irrefutable knowing, that I had lived out Demeter's role and finally understood exactly what 'myth' was—in Jean Houston's words 'something that never was and always is.' The archetypes are living parts in an ongoing drama in which we participate for a while, and then, older and wiser (we hope) leave the role for someone else to experience. Dr. Shinoda Bolen propelled my studies into the mythologies of different times and cultures and I discovered that the story of Inanna from Sumerian mythology was most likely the source for the more familiar myth of Demeter and Persephone.

I recognized Inanna's tale as a living truth. Being stripped bare by the abduction of my son, I had visited the underworld of darkness and depression and experienced a spiritual death. With the unswerving love of my husband and daughter I re-emerged, slowly, oh so slowly. I remember in those dark days, questioning 'God' as I ruminated on the story of Abraham being asked to sacrifice his son. In spite of what I had been experiencing, my response was an affirmation of my faith and trust in some non-gendered Divine Source, 'out there' that I did not understand but to whom, in my heart and soul, I was committed. Irrespective of the suffering I felt, nothing would sever my connection and faith in an unnamed and unknowable mysterious wholeness.

Was it the *Shechina*—the feminine face of Oneness that accompanied me on my journey and never left my side? In appreciation and recognition, my soul work in the second half of my life is a continuing search for The Sacred Feminine, to experience, express and embrace Her energy in all that I do, in an effort to bring balance into our human journey as spiritual beings. For me, the creative source of All That Was, Is and Shall Be is neither masculine nor feminine but how we name, label or interpret Divinity describes our own level of spiritual maturity.

Once we find our way back into the light, we return to life and family, not as we entered into the darkness, but rather as empowered warriors of The Sacred Feminine. My return took years to manifest in the change of direction of my life's work. My discovery of, and union with, women's spirituality as my own, needed to take expression in my own words and images that could be shared.

I saw how my story affected and empowered others in a way that was healing. I also knew that it did not end there but that in bringing together the masculine and feminine energies, we were completing the work of *tikkun olam*—the reparation of our little part and place in the grand scheme.

In retrospect, I remembered that when I was in my early twenties, still living in South Africa and attending an introduction to Kabbalah, we were invited to think of the one question we would ask God if we had the chance. As I think back, it astounds me to recall as clearly as if it happened yesterday, I knew I would ask about the balance of masculine and feminine energies in the world. This came from an unconscious longing deep within my psyche as I had no conscious awareness at that point in my life of women's herstory. It is a great example of being careful what we wish for... or was this a prescience of my soul's plan and commitment for this lifetime?

The journey to wholeness that we each experience is both painful and fruitful. Isn't that what life's polarities are all about? Once we remember who we are, standing in our full authenticity, there is no going back. Becoming all we were meant to be, we change the future story of humanity, by example, by our actions and our evolving consciousness.

The Tree of Inanna
Liliana Kleiner

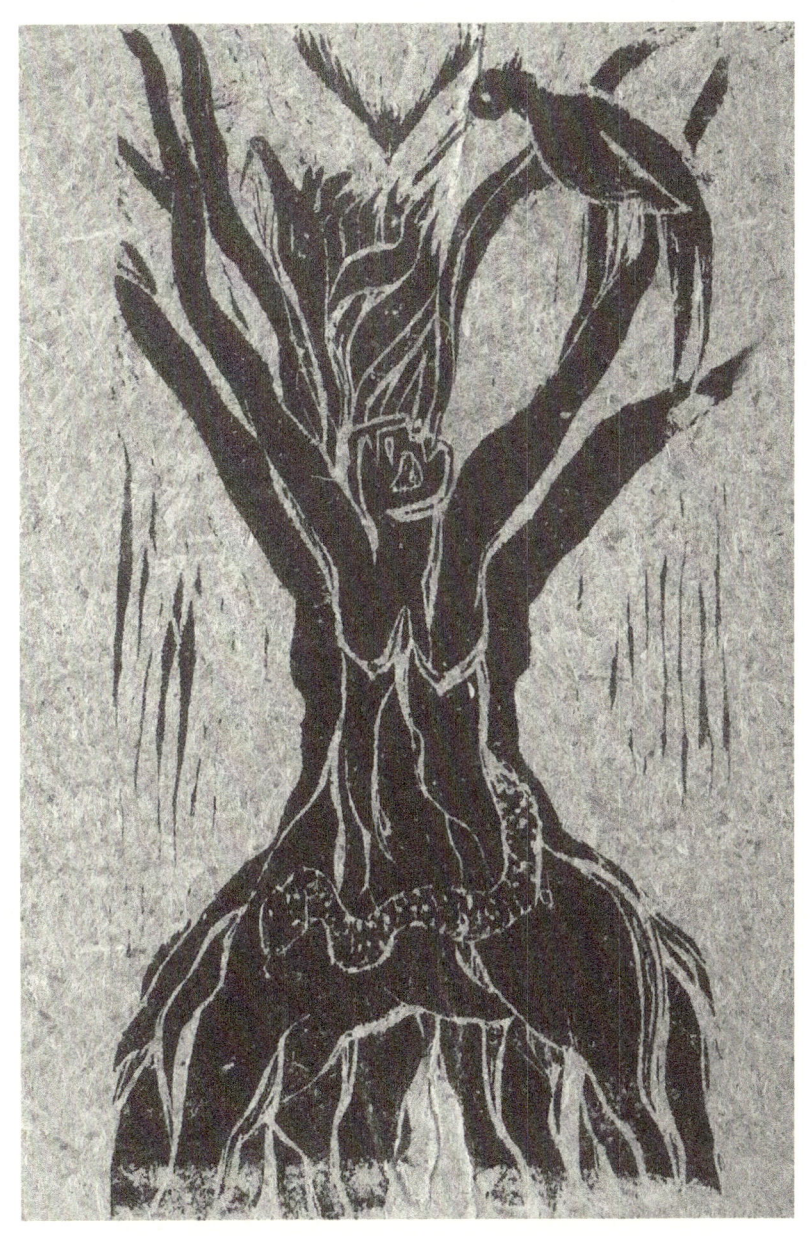

Painting from *The Song of Inanna*.

A Dive into Darkness to Become the Light
Jaclyn Cherie

My love affair with darkness began at birth; I was born with death as company and lungs roaring with rebellion.

Not even for my entry into this world did I stick to the script; a theme that continues throughout my life.

For my entire childhood and most of my Maidenhood, I didn't understand or appreciate the heaviness I carried; not understanding that heaviness would bring me to depths in the collective and my personal psyche most people can't fathom.

Society merely skims the surface remaining shallow.

I didn't know then that my ability to face darkness and bring it to light is a gift.

I didn't know then that my ability to turn wounds into eloquently worded weapons is another gift.

And, I didn't know that my fearlessness when it comes to voicing my opinions as a Woman is yet another gift.

You can't teach courage. You can't teach strength. You can't teach rebellion.

You can't teach someone to be anything other than themselves; their inherent nature will always exist.

Their inherent nature will always win.

The only things you can teach are how to use strengths and faults to become better, to be better, to do better; anything else is futile —people are who they are.

And people can only see as far outside as they have gone inside; the journey must start within.

My outlook on life wasn't always like this though, and it took a couple of Dark Nights of the Soul to help shift my view.

One Dark Night stands out in my memory more than the others; this is not to say that the other Dark Nights were easy, or less traumatic, it just means the one I am speaking of changed the entire direction of my life.

Not that my life had much direction, but after my dance with darkness in 2012-2013 my life had a destination, and I had a newfound purpose.

And, this sudden set course, and deep rooted desire for more out of life was all because I hit rock bottom, almost died, and had to claw my way back up.

It's amazing the fire that burns in one's Soul when the Warrior is called to action, and self-preservation required.

Up until this point the Goddess didn't really exist in my life, or my Craft.

I mean, I had Hekate around and was beginning to experience my nights in the forest with Baba Yaga, but other than those two, there was no real Feminine inspiration of the otherworldly kind.

I didn't know how much I was missing out on.

I didn't know how much that power, that raw Feminine creative power the Goddess embodies, was going to change everything. On my path I had worked with deities and Archetypes that matched how I viewed myself: dark.

I am filled with rage, it's my most natural state of being, and can be (if left uncontrolled) a very toxic emotion.

I am filled with Shadows of trauma and pain that began at birth and didn't stop. Hasn't stopped.

When I thought of my emotions and experiences, they were Masculine and Daemonic. It's amazing how we perceive ourselves even in a Magickal and/or Spiritual context because of the lies Patriarchy tells us.

"Women can't be angry. Women can't be enraged. Women should be pretty, sit up straight, cross their legs, nod in agreement. Don't forget to smile."

Rather than,
"Women can be whatever they want, and angry is definitely something they should be. Be comfortable in your skin, sit however the fuck you want, firmly plant your feet into the ground because they will try and shake you, question authority, be defiant and smile knowing there is a Beast within."

I had always thought of myself as being a "girl's girl" but I only ever encountered mean girls. This didn't deter me from speaking out on Women's issues or calling myself loudly and proudly a Feminist; from my perspective, mean girls are Women with wounds left unaddressed. They're the ones who need Sisterhood more than anyone.

I had several very strong female role models in my life; our family is very much a Matriarchy. But, I moved away from them, from that central community, at the age of 12.

Then it was only my Mom, myself and "the abuser" for 10 years. A prison sentence I will never forget.

I don't regret the move though, because I wouldn't be who I am now at 33, if I didn't experience all the trauma, abuse and Soul Wounds inflicted on me; I do sometimes wonder what I would be like if I had stayed. Who would I be? Would I be as rebellious? Would I be as brave? Would I be as strong?

I believe strength is part of my nature, but it wasn't fully awakened until I was forced into survival mode at a very young age. I don't think any child should have to experience what I did, but I don't resent the experiences anymore either; I'm grateful for them.

I'm grateful for them even when my C-PTSD is triggered, even when anxiety is illogically telling me I am not safe, and my fight or flight is turned on and I can't control my thoughts or emotions. I'm especially grateful when I am sitting in the abyss facing my darkness and turning it into something beautiful.

Something worthwhile.

That probably sounds fucked up to say, and I know Freud would have a field day with it, but it's true.

Pain and trauma are extraordinary teachers; they're the Universe in its most basic yet complex form.

My hysterectomy in 2012/2013 (it had to be done in two steps) was loss on a level I still cannot put into words.

And, it has been my greatest teacher.

That loss is how I was introduced to the Dark Goddess, Crone power, and my Beloved Inanna.

Besides the hysterectomy, I was fresh out of an abusive relationship, recently had a back injury that resulted in my Kundalini awakening and had went thought a mental breakdown; there was a lot going on and I was lost in the darkness with nowhere to turn.

Spiritually, emotionally, mentally and physically I was breaking; my Soul was dying.

One night while in the throes of pain and emotional anguish, I cried so hard for so long that I didn't have anymore tears to shed, so I wept silence and then I slept.

I slept for days.

During my days of sleep, I was accompanied by a Goddess and a lion, a huge majestic lion, in a field of gold as far as the eye could see. There was golden grass, and clouds, golden dirt and animals; it was a Magickal place.

There was the sound of rushing water that called to me through the golden trees, I know it now by name, the crisp blue waters of Creation: the waters of Apsu. I would later experience firsthand its healing powers in a baptism of water and darkness.

A Goddess who was also gold with crimson lips and eternally flowing hair the color of night became my guide. I came to know her as Inanna.

It was She who helped me re-connect to my womb space; she reminded me that I am still Woman even without my organs. She reminded me of the power of my pussy.

She taught me that I was worthy, and that within the void of womb there was endless wisdom to be tapped into.

Inanna reminded me of my sexual nature, my divine Feminine power, and my birthright to be a Mother through other ways than birthing my own children or becoming a Mom in a similar capacity.

She gave me permission to become a Creatrix and my career was child number one.

When discussing Inanna, not many other people see her as a Torchbearer, or a Lightbringer as I do, but for me, that's exactly what She is.

Inanna came to me when I had lost sight of who I was. She came to me in times of darkness with Her golden lessons and ignited a spark inside of me; I turned that spark into a wildfire and that's how my torch came to be.

That very torch is what guides like Souls to me, to my blog, and my books.

It's the torch I carry that reminds me even in the darkest of nights, there is still light, and that light exists inside of me.

Inanna taught me the Alchemical process of turning trauma and pain into golden threads of wisdom and beauty; with these threads I can weave not only my destiny, but I am able to help others see their own inherent divinity.

We are the light in the darkness.

Everyday Inanna
Molly Remer

*The spirit of adventure
runs through my veins
with the rich color
of crushed raspberry
May it always run so free
may it be blessed
and may I be reminded
of the courage and love
shown in small, wild adventures...*

A friend once laughed to hear me describe picking wild raspberries as a "holy task," but it is. A task earthy, embodied, mundane, and miraculous at once. Each year, I sweat and struggle, am scratched and stung, but I return home once again with my bounty.

Several years ago I wrote about my "Inanna's descent" as I picked wild raspberries with my children:

> *As I returned, red-faced, sweating, and after having yelled much more than I should and having said several things I instantly regretted, I was reminded of something that I manage to forget every year: One definition of insanity is picking wild berries with a toddler. In fact, the closest I ever came to spanking one of my kids was during one of these idyllic romps through the brambles when my second son was three. While still involving some suffering, this ramble was easier since I had a nine and a half year old as well as the toddler. This time, my oldest son took my toddler daughter back inside and gave her a bath and put her in new clothes while I was still outside crawling under the*

deck in an effort to retrieve the shoes and the tiny antique ceramic bluebird that my girl tossed over the railing and into the thorns "for mama."

While under the deck, I successfully fished out the shoes (could not find the tiny bird) and I found one more small handful of raspberries. Since the kids were all safely indoors, I took my sweaty and scratched up and irritable self and ran down to my sacred sanctuary in the woods. I was thinking about how I was hot, tired, sweaty, sore, scratched, bloody, worn, and stained from what "should" have been a simple, fun little outing with my children and the above prayer came to my lips. I felt inspired by the idea that parenting involves uncountable numbers of small, wild adventures. I was no longer "just" a mom trying to find raspberries with her kids, I was a *raspberry warrior*. I braved brambles, swallowed irritations, battled bugs, sweated, swore, argued, struggled, crawled into scary spaces and over rough terrain, lost possessions and let go of the need to find them, and served as a rescuer of others. I gave my blood and body over to the task.

Like Inanna, I faced thorny gates and descended into darkness, crawled on my knees, and gave up things that I cherished, and in the process, discovered things about myself—and then returned with a renewed sense of purpose and an awareness of my own strengths.

Fast forward several years as I set out to make homemade marshmallow fondant icing for our daughter's fifth birthday party. My goal: to make little fondant pandas for her birthday cake. I began with my two pounds of powdered sugar, my melted marshmallows, and my all-natural $12 jar of black food pigment. As I kneaded and kneaded the stiff and difficult dough, my journey became more arduous. I ended up yelling at my lovely children who were leaning over my shoulders to watch the adventure unfold. I said, "just get out of the kitchen!" to the birthday girl herself and I hollered for my now 12-year-old to come peel the one-year-old away from my legs as he attempted to scale my body and reach my arms while my hands were covered with black-icing cement. I ranted and raved briefly about how this is an example of my own life-long tendency to overdo and over-perform. Making these pandas wasn't necessary. *I do it to myself.* Why do this to myself, I lamented over and over. What is the point? What am I teaching my kids—the cost of having fun and doing something nice and neat for each other is yelling and feel strained and tense? Why didn't I just buy lard-frosting, I lamented (meaning hydrogenated oil frosting from the store). Why aren't we eating Chicken McNuggets and a cake from Wal-Mart right now? Wouldn't that be better than yelling at my kids and forcing myself to spend hours kneading panda dough? Shouldn't we eat frozen taquitos and watch TV all day and never, ever invite anyone to come to a birthday party ever again?

Then, I fell into a rhythm with the fondant. The sugar started to incorporate. The black started to knead in. I could see it coming together. This is a Hero's Journey, I thought, this is an Inanna's Descent. I heard the call to adventure, or fondant, as it were, and I answered. I set forth with my tools and my optimism. I was challenged on my journey. I came face to face with my own shadows. My fingernails became stained with effort. I cast away expectations and judgments. And, then I started to emerge, coming back from my trek, bearing my prize, carrying my treasure, offering my sweet elixir to my people. When I realized it was actually going to work, I started to feel a sense of exhilaration and glee. It is *empowering* to make your own dang fondant. I called out to my husband with a slightly wild bark of laughter, this is another one of those small adventures! *Parenting involves hero's journeys and Inanna's Descents every day.* What if I'd given up when the fondant got tough? Doesn't that teach my kids to quit, to not bother, to not learn, experiment, do, and try? I thought about giving birth to my children—how the going gets difficult, how you feel like giving up, and then you emerge, tender and strong, a new human in your arms. *I did that! I can do anything!* My parenting is stronger, richer, and deeper from knowing that I can face difficult tasks and do them anyway, from knowing that I can draw upon my own strength, my own body wisdom, my own power, and succeed. I am a better person, a better mother, for having hit my own limit and then, incredibly, realizing I could go beyond it—that I actually still had the will and courage left in me to do it. Those pandas, while less earth-shaking and life-changing than giving birth to children, were born from my own love and effort into my black-icing hands, and my willingness to *do it myself*, for the ones I love.

I've said before that I'd rather be the mom that does cool and fun stuff with her kids and sometimes yells while doing it than a mom who doesn't yell, but who doesn't do cool stuff because she's afraid she might yell or worse yet, because she doesn't have any fun ideas. (Of course, an awesomer option, would be to be the mom who does cool stuff and also doesn't yell, but I'm not holding my breath on that one!) After I constructed the first tiny panda and seeing how cute it was and how excited my daughter was about her cake, I felt such a sense of thrill and triumph. I thought that if I hadn't decided to do it and make it easier on myself, sure, I wouldn't have yelled, but I also wouldn't have felt the empowering sense of having done exactly what I imagined doing. When you do hard things and encounter shadows and keep going and come out the other side, you are strengthened. You learn something about yourself. You realize your own capacities and power. If you are unwilling to embark, you stay safer, and maybe even are a nicer person, but you do not experience the overwhelming satisfaction of accomplishment. The pairing—the difficulty with the triumph—is what makes the journey worth it. This is it, I told my husband, this is The Return. I have returned to my people and I come bearing bears. It feels good to be home.

I am a Priestess of the Goddess
Patricia Ballentine

My sacred work draws me
Down raw dark corridors
Thru jagged doorways
Into seething vessels
Overflowing with the potential
For transformation only found
In the deepest depths of dysfunction and pain.

I am a Priestess of the Goddess

My regalia is frayed at the seams
With unrepaired snags and tattered cuffs
From the constant clawing
Of resistant illusions
So deeply engrained
In destructive beliefs and habits
Ripe for the harvest to good.

I am a Priestess of the Goddess

I walk in rugged boots
With soles worn thin
From the shards of broken hopes and dreams
That litter the pathway
Sometimes bringing me to my knees
In order to see more clearly
The remnant of the passion still present.

I am a Priestess of the Goddess
I am an unlikely servant
In an inhospitable environment

That incubates the most courageous beings
On the threshold of quantum healing
Through courageous acts of self reclamation
Compassion for others
And the elimination of the shackles of fear.

Strength from Shadow

Susan Morgaine

Descent. Powerful Descent.

In a lifetime, how often do we descend? Are we always aware of it?

I am of the mind that I started a descent on the day I was born, when my mother gave me to my grandmother. My initial descent of abandonment and neglect was stopped, temporarily, before it really got started. Living with, and be truly loved by, my grandmother saved my life; even years later, I believe this. I stayed with this beautiful woman until she passed through the veil. Descent re-commenced. At the age of seven, with her death, I learned true loss and overwhelming grief. I went to live with my mother and her partner, always realizing on some level that I was interfering with the life my mother wanted to lead. Each time it was possible to send me away for a period of time, I was.

I was alone. I was lonely. I was in pain. Does the pain of being left and ignored time and again outweigh the pain of not being here? Does the fear and pain you feel as the knife is held to your throat outweigh the calm afterward? Does that pain outweigh the feeling of the pain you feel as you watch yourself drag the piece of glass across your wrist at the age of 13? Does it outweigh the pain of seeing so much blood, panicking and running to clean yourself up, thinking someone is going to notice this, but no one does.

Pain—and descent.

There is the descent of medical illnesses and surgeries, each time control of your body is wrested from you and you begin the descent, and each time you claw yourself back up, refusing to give up, always fighting.

There is the descent that comes with the pain of anxiety, sometimes out of control, when you look at your life and the only thing that stops you from ending it is the love you have for your children.

There is the descent that comes with the pain of family and friends who betray, intentionally and purposefully.

There is the descent that comes with loss, both physical and emotional.

We, each of us, has our pain, our own descent.

While many people suffer and descend throughout their lives via depression, anxiety, loss, I believe that the involuntary descent of a woman (versus the voluntary descent of spiritual growth, which is so different) is that much worse because, more often than not, we suffer in silence, we hold our pain close to our souls. We are taught to not complain, and if we do, many times the words are not heard; and so, our pain is quiet, heard only by ourselves. This is what women learn, this is how we are socialized. No matter what happens, the only thing you truly must do is... smile.

But, somehow we go on, don't we? Through the pain and the anguish. Through the descent and the ascent following. We leave something of ourselves behind each time we fall, only to pick ourselves up and begin again. Each time we leave something behind, something stronger takes its' place, because it must.

The Descent
Arna Baartz

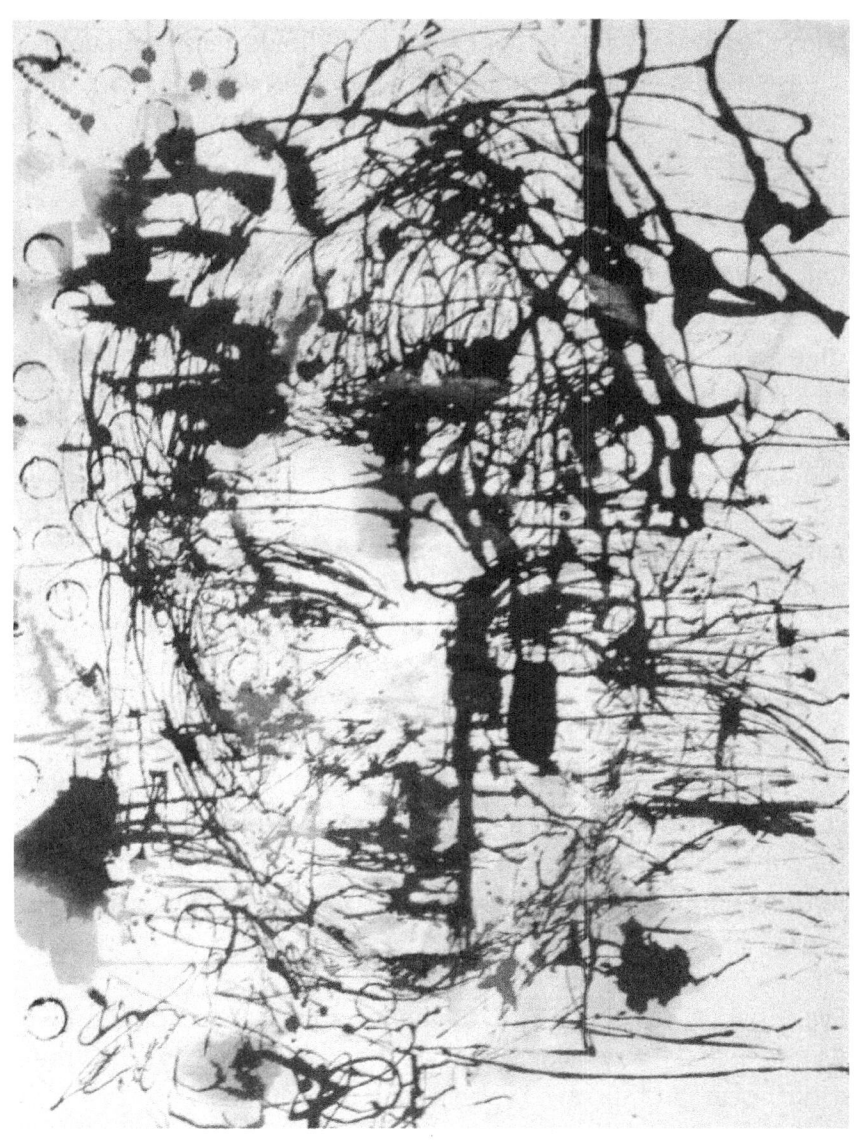

Illustration from *My Name is Inanna*.

Seeking Oracles
Donna Snyder

She gazes at the flame between her eyes, holds her breath until she is nothing but heart, the world's pulse between her ears. She finds black feathers at her doorstep, unsure if the augury is good or ill. Each night she folds her legs and disappears into the sacred fire. She greets the sunrise with a sigh.

Voices echo conversations on eschatology and doom. She hides from them behind guitars' excruciating sweet. Words repeat themselves perpetually in silence. She sees pictures on the wall where there are none.

She knows little of souls but talks to the dead, visits them in their tombs inside her body. Somewhere outside her head, the smell of palo santo smolders. Somewhere, the sounds of hard wind through metal and water dripping. Floorboards creak and a door closes, of their own accord. She never knows whether her ghosts linger, or if she binds them to her, refusing to let them go.

In her sleep, she wraps herself in sheets like Lazarus. When she wakes, she arises from the grave into a world of dust and blinding sun, the desert heat a shroud. There are no dreams here, just her third eye ablaze. She dresses in the memory of rain. Her hair a burning nimbus, her reflection falls into the caves beneath her eyes.

Everything is bleached as coyote bones in this landscape she wanders, and every living thing has thorns. The path is full of rock, forlorn scat, and sorrow. Everyday she trips and falls.
When the flame fades she returns to now, along with ordinary sight. The flicker of candles glows on the other side of her eyelids. The sound of heartbeat subsides and that of barking dogs and

sirens resume. She realizes the music had been inside her head, as had the desert, the thorns, and the talking dead.

Live by the Sun, Love by the Moon
Carolina Miranda, OCT, M.Ed.

There are two forces of motion in the universe. One propels everything to move forward, progressing in a linear way, and the other is circular, ample and recurrent, and what gives us the pace for life. I believe that what we call the Goddess lives in these forces of Time that are circular—the Moon, the Earth revolving around the sun... And so in order for us to understand Time, we need to refine our perception of our life experiences and be attuned to the fine cycles of life in our own lives. What you are about to read is a story of becoming aware of this force, and how I chose to story it or code it on my own body and in the art form of tattooing.

I met Mirabel Lasher in March of 2014—as soon as I managed to put my life back on a good path from a divorce that left me very lost for awhile. I was in full forward motion at the end of January 2014, and that's when I began to think about getting an old tattoo covered. The old tattoo related to my failed marriage and my ex-husband, and I knew in a matter of days as I put my focus on it, exactly what I wanted to replace it with.

I wanted a turtle. A beautiful, powerful, and yet delicate turtle that embodied earthiness, and it also served as a reminder that I can only thrive in clear waters—that I need to stay on a path of integrity and follow my truth. It was also an incredibly powerful image for someone whose identity is so rooted into being a Mother. According to North American Indigenous mythology and traditional tales, Turtles are the Creators, the Mothers of all living things. I wanted to pull that power from the depths of my being and let it flow to the outside of me.

A Google search led me to a few different tattoo shops here in the urban area of Waterloo Region in Ontario, Canada and that's how I came across Mirabel's bio for the first time. I can tell you this: I knew she was the "one," my tattoo artist, without ever looking at her portfolio. That's right: I read her bio – "female South American tattoo artist and also a mom." I knew she would get me, and honour my story, and that she would come through for me. I never saw a drawing, and I booked my appointment with her right away.

After a few first drawings, and some back and forth, I was there in no time to get it done. The drawing we had finally arrived at was amazing, and everything I had unconsciously thought it would be. It incorporated the tree of life I used to wear around my neck with my daughters' names on it. Mirabel was also everything I had thought she was going to be. She is feminine, powerful, unapologetic, a fierce and loving mother, and she has this impressive (and hilarious) collection of phallic-related items. She is that kind of woman that exudes sensuality, sexuality, and female power—all of which she is in full control of.

During our appointment, she told me about her loving husband, and how he doesn't have a any tattoos. She told me about how supportive he has been of her, and her choices, and how he loves her body, which is almost entirely covered in ink. We talked about life, my life and hers, and about our search for meaning, and purpose. She told me about how hard she and her husband work in order to raise a son who will become a good man, educating him to be kind, respectful of women. She adores her little boy.

When we were done and I looked in the mirror, I realized that there was even more meaning to my turtle than I had originally intuitively arrived at earlier. Seeing the finished product, jolted my memory to Ubatuba, the gorgeous beach I spent most of my summers from the time I was 12-years-old. The coast of Ubatuba is my favorite place on Earth, and where I still go every time I go to Brazil. It is home to one of the biggest sea-turtle conservation projects in the country, Projeto Tamar. Sea turtles, as only deep memory could have revealed, were truly a part of my childhood experiences. They had always been there, but I had to re-discover them by activating that deep memory through intuition, cautiously re-discovering my own story.

I said good-bye to Mirabel, swearing I would never come back. This had been a very painful two and a half hours, and I was not really into tattoos that much to want to have any more ink done. She smirked, in a way that only Mirabel can smirk. She knows her art, and she knows people. I am pretty sure she knew, before me, that I would be back in no time.

As my story developed, I was back to the shop a second time around just within a few months, to get a damselfly done. A damselfly that earned her way into my body by showing up in one of the most mystical experiences I've had around memory and healing. In the summer of 2014, I decided to reclaim another part of my story by revisiting a site I had almost died at seven years earlier. I went on a hike with my parents at the Elora Gorge in Ontario, and during that hike I stared at a cliff that I had almost fallen from. I had decided to get over a very old trauma related to sexual manipulation and abuse. Years earlier, I had been drugged and left wandering that site on my own at night, and this left me dealing with panic attacks for two years. As I put myself on a path of healing and openness in 2014, I found myself trying to reclaim the spaces that had once felt hostile to me in a way that also felt safe and healing. During my hike, my body gravitated to the rock that I had almost fallen from seven years earlier, instinctively. I didn't know if I would be able to find it or identify it, but the shiver in my spine was undeniably an indicator of a site that I remembered far too well again, through deep memory. As I carefully approached the rock, a damselfly landed on it and it stayed there, staring back at me: almost as if reminding me of my strength, that I had survived, and that we had both transformed.

Again, I don't believe in randomness. I believe our intuition is deeply aligned with collective wisdom and memory. And so every time I come across something that feels like a clear sign toward the path I should be on, I do my due diligence, and I try to understand its cultural meaning. Damselfly / Dragonfly's Medicine in North American Indigenous cultures include the Mastery of life on the wing, power of flight, power to escape a blow, understanding dreams, power of light, breaking down illusions, seeing the truth in situations, swiftness, change, connection to Dragon, transcendence, winds of change, wisdom and enlightenment. Dragonflies yield the message that life is never what it appears to be. This is a power animal which can help to put us in touch with nature spirits.

And so on I went to Mirabel again, in the Fall, to story this moment onto my skin, so that I would always remember it, moving forward in my life with the landmarks that would allow me to revert to the most intimate and meaningful memories of trauma and healing.

The next tattoos—yes—there were two more as the story goes, were a hibiscus flower, and a sun in the shape of a spiral—all of which as it turns out, were linked by the thread of one much bigger story. Each with their own beautiful story, each with their own precise meaning, coming together slowly, to form a major work of art on my body which in time has revealed its major purpose: They represent the four classic elements of nature (water, air, earth, fire). Perhaps not by chance, as some people have in fact called me a force of nature. As the drawings came to life, my connection to Mirabel deepened, and I also had the privilege and the honour to get to know her and at least a part of her story, which was as much a part of this adventure as any of my tattoos, or my stories.

So on March 11th 2015 at 4:30 PM, there I was again, getting my two new tattoos done: the hibiscus flower and the spiral sun. This time we got talking about family, religion, raising children, marriage, relationships, and sex… We talked about how she feels she has gotten sexier since she turned 40, and she believes it's related to her wild beautiful long hair (several different traditions and cultures in the world show a very clear relationship between spirituality and hair, including North American First Nations, which has taught me so much about the land, and about the universe through its cosmology).

Mirabel also told me about how she knew she was going to be a tattoo artist at the age of 12. She said she saw a photo of an older woman on a *National Geographic* cover, and that she was covered in tattoos. Mirabel says that right then, at that very moment, she knew what she was going to do. There was no doubt in her mind or any question – she was completely attracted to that art form, and she knew that was her path and what she was meant to create. I believe we actually do know. Deep inside, and early on, who we are. We just forget because of the world we've created, and our lack of touch with our own story.

We talked about immigration and how coming to Canada was not an easy move for her family. Her family moved to Ontario from Uruguay, where life was simple and yet, they had everything. She was about seven-years-old, and she said they struggled financially here in Canada; life was just hard. But she stuck to a good path, finished school and became an artist and she's glad she did, because this is what saved her sanity from the biggest hardship she's ever endured so far: the early loss of her mother, Luz Marina (a name which is precious by the way, it means Light from the Sea).

Her mom, as Mirabel describes her, was "the real deal." She was the powerful one, the intuitive matriarch: strong, beautiful and fearless. Mirabel lost her mother at 26 and it was through tattooing people and in many ways by becoming a part of people's own stories and healing with them that kept her going (as she explained to me, many tattoos are memorials to loved ones). Every time Mirabel talks about her mother, it's like something magical lights up inside of her – Luz appears—she lights up. She has said it more than once: "I think I am always going to be living under my mother's shadow, and that's OK by me, because my mom, man.. She was pretty amazing."

So when I came by this last time, I decided to bring her a good-bye gift. I knew our work of art had come full cycle, and this was indeed probably the last time I was going to see Mirabel in the shop, for a while anyway. I bought her Cheryl Strayed's book, *Wild*. When she saw the book her reaction was priceless: She looked at me and said, "Wow! I am going away for March break with my son and I was totally thinking of asking you the name of that book you were reading when you last came here for the damselfly. This is actually pretty wild! Thanks."

I smiled, and kept watching her finish up my hibiscus tattoo, observing her talk to her buddy that had just dropped in to get her opinion on a tattoo he was working on. That's when I said, "You know Mirabel... This feels awfully familiar.. I think we are truly arriving at the end of a full cycle here because I feel it was almost a year ago that I came over to the shop for the first time. It was definitely around March Break, I remember that..." As a teacher, March Break is a defining marker of time for me. That's when I had an idea and said: "Hey, actually let's see, I have my phone so why don't I check? I keep everything on my phone these days, so I am sure we can figure out if this weird feeling I am having has anything to it for real. It does feels weird and special in a way..."

Lo and behold, I go back to my calendar and there it was: Exactly a year ago, on March 11, 2014 at 4:30PM I had walked into the shop for the very first time. An exact year to the calendar date had passed since we had first met each other. I showed it to her because although this happens to me far more often than not, I still get chills in my spine and find it hard to believe each and every time. Perfect cycles. All she could say was "This is fucked!" We both paused quietly staring at one another, shaking our heads. She had stopped tattooing too. For that brief moment, all we could do was shake our heads, laugh, stare, and breathe. Then she said it again now in true awe: "Dude, this is totally fucked!"

It was.

It felt insane, sacred, beautiful, and bonding. It also made me think that if we stay open and allow things to happen, then the universe does flow. We shared a big, loud, unapologetic laugh and that is when I saw it clearly. The angle of the story that only someone looking at her and really seeing her, can actually understand – like a prism. I realized what Mirabel may not have seen or understood yet: that she doesn't have to worry about living under her mother's shadow because it is precisely her mother's light, and the light and the fire of the women that have come before her even, that beam right through Mirabel's eyes, as she lights up the way for so many more.

As for the rest of my story, time went by, I began to fully understand and embrace the power of what I like to call the Goddess, and how it relates to a fuller account of life through Time, encompassing the circular movement of the universe that is responsible for nurturing everything that is alive, and giving its cyclical order. I was brought up in a Catholic tradition, oblivious to my Indigenous heritage. The more I learn from the North American First Nations, the more I have reconnected with the ways of knowing that value Time that is non-linear, and non-solar. Catholicism and the Gregorian calendar has established metrics and Time through the Sun. It completely ignores however the metrics of the moon, or of our galaxy, all of which moves circularly.

My love of mythology, history and education led me to finding out that different cultures around the world had always different versions of their interpretation for this cyclical movement. Inanna, Ishtar, IxChel—these were all entities that were worshiped well before patriarchy took on the world like a virus. Each of these Goddesses are particular to their own local geographic region, but they hold the same essence: They are the goddesses of love, beauty, sex, desire, fertility, war, combat, justice, and political power. This was the way ancient civilizations found to interpret these powerful forces of nature and which all relate to the sacred Feminine. The more comfortable I have become with understanding what this Goddess really means in a rational manner, through physics, mythology, history, cosmology—and looking at it from a strictly educational perspective—the easier it has become to embrace its essence in a spiritual way.

In 2017, for my 37th birthday, I decided to go to Iroquoi Ink here at the Ohsweken First Nations Reserve, and get a full chest tattoo of the Mayan Goddess IxChel. IxChel was the Mayan Goddess who holds a similar mythology to that of Inanna. I have become comfortable with displaying Her proudly on my chest despite being an educator in a conservative Catholic system. I have also since began to reclaim my Indigeneity, and although I can no longer associate myself with any particular tribe or land as I was severed from it three generations ago, I can proudly say that I am a woman who understands the power of the moon, and of cyclical time, and of relationships, all of which are so vital to life and to the care all Indigenous cultures have shown to the Earth.

I plan on reviving this knowledge as much as I can in a renewed way, while I continuing to study sciences, creating new mythology through the knowledge I have of nature and philosophy. I am no longer willing to live in a world where we continue to glorify Sons and worship the Father figure only. As a devoted and strong Daughter of this incredibly life giving planet, the land guides me and I have taken on as my life mission and commitment to elevate and hold the figure of the Mother, as a Creator of equal status of power.

Inanna Advises Her Initiate
Psyche North Torok

One day, you will make the journey
into the belly of *should*,
into the cauldron of *not good enough*,

into the gut of *unworthy*.
Neither gods nor darkness will show mercy.
Shadows will carve your life.

Desire will drop away, begging survival.
Try any means to avoid it;
still you will be called to your descent,

your muscles spent, leaden,
your thoughts embalmed in silence.
Take with you what you may;

you will lose it all.
But leave one jewel here –
the best you have – to pull you home.

Bury it on some wild hilltop.
Bury it by your oldest cedar.
Bury it in the roots of your heart:

One gem to draw you back to
yourself, potent as a secret,
unwavering as the underworld.

Shield For The Fiery Path
Patricia Ballentine

Black & White 2018.

Venus Direct as Inanna's Ascent:
The Empress Enthroned

Nuit Moore

Back on September 6th, 2015, Venus went direct in Leo after a 40-day stretch of retrograde—a retrograde that embodied the Underworld descent and ascent journey of the Goddess Inanna/Ishtar—the Lady of the Star, Venus Herself. Goddess of Sexual Love and also of Royal Power. She cries of not just ecstasy, but also of war.

Having an intensely intimate experience with the mythos of the Lady—having already undergone and surviving a 14-year journey of descent and ascent—I had decided with that retrograde that I would personally holy-hermit through that transit via my energetic withdrawal from the active machinations of the chaos of desire and power control in the context of relationships. I told myself that I would seek sacred solitude and wrestle my lions, for they had been wild within me, fierce with roar and roam. For the lion is associated with Inanna/Ishtar—is in fact, her animal totem of power and majesty—and I was not feeling fully in mastery of myself. But in order to do so, I had to surrender to the journey. I had decided, in essence, to be the Magdalene[29] in the Wilderness—my own 40 days and 40 nights to look my temptations—those fiercely roaring, roaming beasts, my own inner war—in the face.... including most intimately the echoes of said beasts deep within my own well. To employ my blessed balm to my own heart scars, to declare myself the Anointed One as I underwent this transformation. In doing so, I could once again claim my seat on the throne of Empress—She who bears the scepter of personal power, and also the shield of Venus, star of Inanna. To see my lions calm with majesty, confident in my power.

---

29 The Magdalene is now thought by many to have been a priestess of the Goddess Inanna. I have long thought this to be true.

It wasn't easy, that transit. Not just for myself, but so many then. It brought especially heavy work at that time for so many of my scarlet sisters—those women walking the scarlet path... Lilith women, Magdalene women, Inanna/Ishtar women. There were deep revelations concerning power in relationships during that transit, as well as with authenticity. Veils were removed, and many of us stood vulnerable with each lost layer—just as Inanna did with each sacrifice made deeper along Her descent. The Venus in retrograde transit of 2015 truly embodied the challenges and treasures found within deep inner heart work. Many of us found that our concepts of relationships had undergone a deep transformation, or an intense validation process. There was heart alchemy on high. Many of us at that time doing the work also found that what we previously considered part of our core authentic self had also undergone the same process of shift and reveal. Self-aspects were released and others discovered (or rediscovered). The work of that transit pulled the veil over our eyes in many ways—including veils we may have self-created as a result of denial or in avoidance of healing certain emotional issues. Many of us found ourselves in our desert wilderness, wrestling with our beasts. Decisions were made to let go of people and situations that had brought only conflict. Conflict can be necessary for growth, but there comes a time when it no longer serves our growth. That transit highlighted that in a major way. The medicine offered was found in release to make way for resurrection—in sacrifice and surrender in order to soar.

To give you an idea of what I personally experienced during that 40-day period, it included the following:

I released a Beloved passion of mine, in the name of Holy Love and sacred sisterhood.

I quickly received crystal clear vision on a sudden 'relationship' that was not at all what it was being presented as, and removed myself from it, ending energetic drain and regaining equilibrium.

I dwelled for a good while in the bitter desert within, in my dark and shadow—and looked my anger, my depression, my despair, my disgust, my deepest losses and my most intense regrets in the face. And I sat with them. I slept with them. I spoke with them. They permeated my dreamscape. Keening dreaming. My psyche keening with the purging, I surrendered... flowing in the Void.

I finally gathered strength to find out how my husband... who was all at once my Dumuzi, my Hades, my Osiris, my Bridegroom... to find out the exact details of his cause of death, and found it was ruled a suicide. Widow mourning fresh as the fields are reaped and the sacrificial gods meet their fate—bringing further release and the compost of rebirth.

And I released a great deal of old trauma tied to my Mother-wound. Taking care of my own inner child without guilt, as I have learned to do.

Intense, needless to say.
Those 40 days of Venus in Retrograde in Leo personally felt like several years worth of wisdom-work.
Serious alchemy. Flame to ash. Descent to ascent.
Empress enthroned. The mastery of the lions, the Queen out of the Underworld.
The Magdalene, back from the desert wilderness, dancing in the Garden.
Her own holy balm on her burns...
the Goddess returns.

The next two Venus in retrograde transit dates are: October 6-November 16th 2018 in Scorpio to Libra, May 13-June 25th 2020 in Gemini. Be aware of what happens during your own 40 days and 40 nights.

Rising II
Chantal Khoury

Graphite and charcoal on mylar, 2017.

Inanna
Lori Newlove

Inanna
Share with us the powers of rebirth

Inanna, Inanna

>Verse:
>Inanna,
>Lady of the moon and dark wild places
>Inanna
>Lapis shining Lady come embrace us
>Inanna
>Lady take your veils into the earth
>Inanna
>Share with us the powers of rebirth
>Inanna, Inanna

Music by Brian Seachrist.
The song can be heard on Youtube.

Shamans vs. Aliens:
Adapting The Descent of Inanna
K. A. Laity

I distinctly remember starting my novel *Owl Stretching*. Kurt Vonnegut had just died and I felt such sorrow that there would be no more funny/sad books in his distinctive voice. So I started writing a book that was funny and sad about an apocalyptic time in the place where I then was (Albany) but in a slightly alternate future (a United States that had lost the Revolutionary War—so had closer ties to the UK but was still not Canada).

I don't know when I decided to use *The Descent of Inanna* as an organizing plan for the novel's arc, but I suspect it was around the time that I was planning my course on Women & Early Writing. In my previous academic position I had covered survey courses, so given everything before 1800 as my remit for the course, I thought, 'Let's go back all the way!' People generally refer to Gilgamesh as the first written text, but I always turn to Inanna as the 'beginning' story. Why settle for bromance when you can have sisters, transformation, drumming, and death?

The course bombed at the start—in the bad way. The students just stared at me, completely lost. I took the unusual step of sitting down and asking them, 'What's going wrong?' I was so excited about showing them how Western culture betrayed the marvelous women of the past, but they just sat there silently. Once they realised I really did want to know what was going on, they told me, 'We have no idea what this is.'

They knew nothing about mythology, they'd never heard of the Sumerians, they had no context for understanding what the descent meant. The students had not even heard of Persephone and Demeter, so that parallel escaped them, too. We started over with a lot more deliberation. 'You don't have to know all the context,' I assured them. 'This is among the oldest stories we have. It's the story of a powerful woman seeking more power, giving up everything she has to find the ultimate secret of death (her shadow self), finally dying—and then discovering that friendship has the power to reach beyond death.'

What did I want them to learn? Trust your friends: They will beat the drum to lead you back.

Having been a drummer for some years, inspired greatly by the late Layne Redmond's *When the Drummers Were Women*, the power of that sound resonated so clearly in my imagination. How do you take care of yourself? Make a plan! Who is your Ninshubur? Who will plead on your behalf, make public lamentations, go to the temples and yes, beat the drum to give you hope? Women are constantly erased—missing, discounted, disparaged, dismissed. We are punished for our ambitions, for wanting more, wanting to know more, daring to have power. But we are strong when we stick together.

Inanna hangs, a wretched corpse on the wall. It is a punishment for her ambition, but it is also a warning from Ereshkigal: Acknowledge and honour your shadow side. Inanna gave up all the symbols of her divinity as she made her way to her sister's realm: her golden crown, all the lapis and garments and objects, the me that reflected her manifold powers. She hangs in darkness for three days like the moon going dark. Alone, bereft, unmade— she is no longer Inanna. Ereshkigal, her mirror self, suffers too. Inanna unmade is a part of herself unmade. In this is the lesson that harming another woman harms ourselves. Both are in misery. When Ninshubar prevails upon Enki to at last send creatures ('galla') to rescue her, they creep into the underworld to take up the position of mourners. They show compassion to the sorrowing goddess Ereshkigal, reflecting her moans of pain, for she is mourning her husband's death, which her sister caused. The galla offer sympathy and empathy—what Inanna ought to have offered. Too often women's sorrow and pain gets dismissed as 'whining' when all we need is to be heard, to be acknowledged. We can come back from the darkness with a little hope and sympathy.

The dark goddess offers her mourners a gift of their choosing. The little creatures ask for the corpse of Inanna. It seems a worthless thing, but Ereshkigal grants it and with the food and water of life, they restore the goddess to herself. Inanna returns to the world above, but death must have its offering. In the end her husband Dumuzi and his sister Geshtinanna each share a season in the land of the dead. It is a debt we all must pay, even a goddess, for death comes to each of us in time.

In my novel, the accidental shaman Ro ends up making that descent, too. Like Inanna, she has at times been careless of others. She has failed to acknowledge their sorrows and suffering, consumed too much by her own mourning. But she has ambitions to power, too, and finds herself willing to risk much in hopes of understanding the forces that have invaded their world. On top of an agricultural blight that has devastated food production across the globe, there has been an invasion of aliens who consume humans.

Another group of aliens—potentially helpful—are trying to make contact mentally, but are having some difficulty connecting to such primitive brains. Ro must go through an ordeal to prepare her mind for the connection. Her descent takes place in shamanic space, but is no less vivid for all that. Despite her isolationist tendencies, the young woman has managed to forge ties strong enough that their drums will bring her back.

Will it be enough to defeat the aliens? Well, you'll have to read the book to find out.

Looking back, I realise that writing the book was a way of healing my own descent into darkness. My first academic job out of grad school was in a place that I found dispiriting on every level. The climate was everything that I hated (heat and humidity) and the political climate just as bad. My partner at the time was struggling too. My response to all the stressors was to double down on work, to write my way out of that job and into a better one.

I did manage it after a few years; we got away. I got a better job in a much more congenial area, where I could step outside the house without immediately collapsing, but everything was not magically fixed. There was still the price to pay for my time in the underworld. My partner was succumbing to the effects of his depression and despite all my efforts, it wasn't on me to 'fix' this problem. Depression is a multi-armed demon. You have to face that shadow yourself. In retrospect, I can see how this novel gave me strength to survive not only the dark journey but all that I had to give up: my image of myself as strong, the relationship that no longer worked, the life we had built together. I got better at allowing people to help me. I am grateful to see my former partner thriving again. I built a new life with friends, lovers and adventures.

And like Dumuzi and Geshtinanna, I live in two places. People find it odd, but my job is in one country and my heart in another. I would be glad to live in the land above all the year, but for now I must spend half my time in the underworld. I do my best to learn from it. After all, the ways of the underworld are perfect, Ereshkigal tells Inanna, they ought not be questioned. I work, I look forward to the return, I beat the drum and again I rise.

Chaos and Creation
Arna Baartz

Illustration from *My Name is Inanna*.

We Were Inanna
Hazel DaHealer

We have all made decisions that caused us to enter a time of darkness. Sometimes seeds of greatness germinate in that darkness. Like Inanna, those seeds rise and through this we bloom.

The decision to marry young sent me into an abyss. I found myself in a physically and mentally abusive relationship that literally almost cost me and my daughter our lives. In my darkest hour I was able to get myself and my young daughter out of danger with the help of loved ones. The only way for me to support us was to go to school and get a degree that would lead to a better paying job with benefits. I enrolled in the local Technical College while working nights and weekends. There was very little sleep and most days were spent working and going to school full time. After several difficult years, like Inanna, I rose.

Success for me now meant that my daughter was safe and we could afford to live in our small home. I now had a college degree, a used car and a much better job. The job was supposed to be a stepping stone to the job I intended to work toward. The job paid better but there was a cost. The cost was heavy for a young single mother. I was frequently reminded of the bad place I had left behind several years ago. I often went back into the abyss of self-doubt and fear of failure as I did the best I could to help others. To this day, now decades later, I don't know how I was able to continue to rise like Inanna.

One uneventful night the phone rings and another young mother is in that painful dangerous place. She is in the process of literally fighting for her life. My horror awoke and once again I was scared but there was no time for fear. Lori was screaming. I could hear her attacker force the door into her home. The brutality is difficult to remember but I must because Lori's story needs to be told. I heard her body slam against the wall. I heard her groans as the knife slashed her face and plunged into her chest. Another person was heard entering the home. The fight continued, there was screaming, bodies crashing through furniture, and terror that words just can't describe. The phone had fallen to the floor in the early stages of the attack. Now there is a rustling sound as the phone is being picked up.

"Hello," says a tiny voice barely audible over sounds of the fight. "Sara," was the answer I got when I asked to whom I was speaking. Sara told me she was four years old and she wanted me to help her Momma. Sara was under the kitchen table in a very small apartment. One of the most difficult things I have had to do was get Sara to quietly answer questions and stay very still so she didn't draw the attention of the attacker.

Sara was scared but like Inanna, she rose. She told me who was hurting her Momma. She told me how much she liked school. I told her help was coming. It seemed like an eternity. I wasn't sure help would get there before she was discovered by the attacker. She asked me what was my name. She asked if I had a little girl. She told me that she liked to paint as someone who is being stabbed very close by is going into respiratory distress. The gurgling continued just like the blows to the body continued as Sara asked if I was coming to help her Momma. Two adults one of which is moaning as the attacker continues now screams for help stopped. The silence is deafening. Sara did as I asked and stayed very quiet. She said the blood from the boo boo was getting on her. I know someone is dying as I tell the child a doctor will come to try to fix the boo boo. The blood from her mother's wounds had reached Sara's hiding spot. My heart sank, there was a lump in my throat. "I need you to stay with me just a little bit longer, help is almost there. "Stay with me Sara," was what I kept repeating.

The sounds of different voices are now heard and I exhale as I realise that help is there and Sara is unharmed. One of my folks is trying to talk Sara out from under the table. "That's my friend Oscar. He is going to help you and Mommy, Sara, go to Oscar." "Hey Sara," says Oscar as he takes the phone from her and disconnects the call after telling me, "I got her."

Immediately after the call was disconnected the line rings again. The new caller asks for me to send someone because of the noise of the basketball bouncing next door is just too much to have to listen to. Yeah, I shifted from nurturing to trying to be professional about the inconsiderate children who are bouncing a ball in their own yard. I had to pee an hour and a half ago and there are no signs of a bathroom break in my near future. Supper wasn't going to happen anytime soon either which was not helping my disposition. I trudged on, there was no rising like Inanna.

Oscar comes in several hours later and tells me that Sara is with her Grandmother, the Mom is in still in surgery and the other person is expected to make a full recovery. He tells me how difficult it was to get to Sara and the other victims due to the floor being slippery because of the amount of blood. The attacker was arrested in the parking lot. I didn't hear anything more about this event until I get a subpoena for court a few years later.

The attacker sat in the courtroom neatly dressed. The defense attorney said in the opening statement that the attack happened but the defendant was fighting for his life. Nausea engulfed me as I sat remembering the call. The prosecutor played the tape of that seven-minute phone call. I got lost reliving that horrible night as the tape played. I wasn't watching the jury or the defendant. All of a sudden, I'm aware of my surroundings as Oscar leaned over and told me to go home. It was over.

I left the courtroom unsure of what had happened. I made the drive home wondering how long Sara and her family would be safe. Would the attacker be convicted, and if so, how long would it take before he carved up his next victim? The next time I saw Oscar he had a big smile on his face. I asked why the trial was stopped. The defense attorney had requested a recess and accepted a plea bargain that sent the attacker to prison for twenty-three years before he would be eligible for parole—rather than face the jury who witnessed Sara's bravery in the face of pure evil. A conviction could have resulted in the death penalty for the attacker.

Sara had literally saved her own life and the lives of two others because she was brave. That four-year-old little girl stopped a monster. Like Inanna, she rose from a place many adults don't escape. Eighteen years have passed and I wonder what damage may linger with Sara because of someone else's bad decisions and actions. It is my hope that she is a well-adjusted young lady who is happy with her life.

Inanna's message for us is that when we rise others will rise with us. Inanna reached out and pulled me from the darkness. I was then able to pull Sara from the darkness. Brave little Sara extended her hand and took her Mom with her from a dark and dangerous place. I don't know how long we will remain in the light before troubled seasons come and once again we sink into the abyss. It's something we all do. We sink and then we rise. May Inanna come again during our troubles and offer her hand so that, again, we rise like Inanna.

Ecstasy
Iriome R. Martín Alonso

Lover Goddess' words

I'm the passion and lust of the huntress maiden; the lovely shape of youth made flesh and the palpitation of the pearls of pleasure in the center of a woman's body.

I'm the shadow under a succulent breast; the soft, heavy shape of small tits before the valley of your womb and the life giving circle of your hips.

I'm the old mountains of a whore's ass and the dark sensitive nipples hard from cold and desire.

I'm the freedom of pleasure and the liberation of orgasm. The ecstasy of a star colliding between your legs making you feel so big, so high, so divine, you become Goddess Herself, reaching heavens while being earth.

I'm the wet tongue of your lover between your lower lips and the salty stream of life among delight.

I'm your fingers when you touch yourself and the way you fuck yourself by looking at your image in a mirror while cuming.

I'm the free spirit, joyful and loving, lust-full, wild and free. The sacred whore and the pure virgin at once.

I am the fuel of life itself.

The Fuel of Life Itself
Arna Baartz

Illustration from *My Name is Inanna*.

Lily's Abortion in the Room of Statues

Annie Finch

Pregnant from a rape, Lily, a young contemporary woman, journeys from San Francisco to Kali's cabin near the Serpent Mound in Ohio. The Kouretes are a chorus of heirophants of the Goddess. This passage is excerpted from *Among the Goddesses: An Epic Libretto in Seven Dreams*.

KOURETES:
We are approaching the Serpent Mound

LILY:
I walk cautiously, knowing my belly
full of wide wings, night, and starlight.
[SHE APPROACHES THE HOUSE. A FLAME SHINES THROUGH A WINDOW.]
I can see her, sitting, sewing
on a huge tapestry.

LILY KNOCKS

Dream 7: Kali

On the shaking and rattling bus
feeling nauseous, I looked for courage.
The other heart had begun its beating
in the rich cave, the long silence,
the hoping morning that had been my womb.
Through my belly ran knife-hard images
to my body and to my heart.
For the first time, the pregnancy hurt me.
I knew its life could betray mine soon.

The hate that had touched me on the mountain
was still thriving, making a silence
deep in me still, a yielding mine,
where my own thoughts could not find a foothold
but plummeted, hopeless, down in my body,
absorbed by its power. I stayed quiet.
Houses started to thin out around me.
Night filled the horizon's undulations,
branching out in darkening trees.

KOURETES:
She stands up slowly.
She puts the tapestry down on the table.

Then the bus stopped. Leaves brushed at the windows.
Rain was coming. I knew through the thick sky
the smell of water, along with dusk.
We were approaching the Serpent Mound,
where an ancient hill made a long grassy snake
coiling hard in the wilding night.
Rain pulled at me with the air of a distance
as the driver opened the door.
Soon I would get out and look for Kali.

With a rattle of strap and backpack,
missing Brigid, I moved to the door
and looked out while we rocked to a stop.
The dark highway led me from the others,
and then a narrow path led to Kali.
Mist soaked my skin, and the night finally entered.
Past the place where the edge of the Mound
was spiralling, I moved through untrimmed branches
wet with rain, to her muddy driveway.

KOURETES:
She stands up slowly.

She puts the tapestry down on the table.
We see in its folds a glimpse of creation,
animals, planets, mountains, and trees,
embroidered thick with contrasts and colors,
on a background as warm as blood.

THE DOOR OPENS. KALI APPEARS THERE, LOOKS AROUND
BLANKLY, AND SHUTS THE DOOR.

I walked cautiously, knowing my belly
full of wide wings, night, and starlight.
Her small light shone like a flame through one window
where I could see her, sitting, sewing
on a huge tapestry. I knocked and waited
in the rain, as she stood up slowly
and carefully put it down on the table.
I saw in its folds a glimpse of creation,
animals, planets, mountains, and trees,
embroidered thick with contrasts and colors,
on a background as warm as blood.

AFTER A MOMENT OF SILENCE, LILY RUNS FORWARD ANGRILY
AND POUNDS ON THE DOOR.

LILY [POUNDING]:
Kali! Kali! Come back out here!
Let me in! Kali! Kali!
KALI, WHO IS VERY SMALL, OPENS THE DOOR AGAIN AND STANDS
THERE STARING AT LILY. LILY MOVES TO STAND BESIDE HER IN THE
DOORWAY. KALI SUDDENLY BRUSHES PAST HER RESENTFULLY.
LILY FOLLOWS HER IN.

Then she opened the door. I was nervous,
and drew back a moment, speechless, waiting
for her to see me. What would she do?
Nothing. All she did was stand there

one long minute, with hollow eyes
in a chiseled face, blind to my body,
look unfocussed, and shut the door.

Gouged and shocked, with those two sharp impressions
shadowing my eyes, where her smudged, sightless vision
had absorbed me, undone me, and left me
as wet as invisible, outside the door,
I half-panicked. I thought of leaving,
but then ran forward in desperate anger
and pounded again on the glistening wood,
shouting, calling, cursing and threatening her
till she finally answered, and focused, and stared.

She stared up and down and stared right through me,
half-attentive and clearly resentful,
while I stood on the doorstep. And then,
when I had followed her purposefully in
and stood beside her, towering past her,
I saw that her tiny face was resigned,
ready to help me. She grew taller,
it seemed, and harder, and I was confused
and drew far back so she could walk by.

Scene 3. Inside Kali's house. The huge tapestry rests on a table at stage left. There is a wall in the center of the stage with a cupboard, painted red with a purple border, and a door leading to another, smaller room which is in darkness so complete it is nearly impossible to see it.

KALI GOES TO A CUPBOARD AND TAKES OUT A TALL JAR FILLED WITH DRIED FLOWERS. SHE TAKES OUT A HANDFUL AND PUTS THEM IN A BOWL WITH SOMETHING FROM ANOTHER JAR. SHE OPENS THE DOOR AND URGES LILY INTO THE SMALL ROOM. LILY SITS ON THE FLOOR WHILE KALI POUNDS AND MIXES UP THE CONTENTS OF THE BOWL, OPENS THE DOOR AGAIN AND PUTS

THE BOWL ON THE FLOOR. SHE GESTURES LILY TO DRINK. LILY
DRINKS IT SLOWLY AND PUTS THE BOWL DOWN. KALI TAKES THE
BOWL AND LEAVES.

Did I have to explain what I wanted?
Did she wait till I tried to explain?
No, of course not; she'd known my story
before I had come. She was Kali;
she stretched now and reached into a cupboard,
painted red with a purple border,
pulled a bowl out, and scooped in something
from a tall jar—it looked like dried flowers,
Queen Anne's lace maybe, though it was crumbled—

Dream 8: Inanna

—and gave it to me. While I held it, she rummaged,
found a jar and poured something else in,
mixed them, gestured me into a room,
closed the door, and left me there in darkness
which soon settled. Then I could see
a whole room full of motionless faces.
Each one was staring. She opened the door,
blinding me, brought in the bowl, and set it
on the floor by my feet, and gestured
for me to drink it. I drank it and coughed.
Before I had finished, she left me again.
In the light, I had seen a mattress,
cushion, and basin laid out on the floor,
and two walls that were full of statuses
resting on shelves, mostly small, but one huge,
towering past me. I stared at her robes,
which I dimly saw now, as darkness
moved in closer for a long night's ordeal.

Scene 4. The left side of the stage goes completely dark, and the room on the right is dimly lit to reveal at least a hundred different statues of goddesses on shelves around the room. One statue of Inanna at the back of the stage is much larger than the others. There are also a mattress, cushion, and basin on the floor.

KOURETES are on the left side of the stage. They begin to chant softly to the traditional tune: "Isis, Astarte, Diana, Hecate, Demeter, Kali--Inanna."

LILY COUGHS. SHE LIES DOWN TO SLEEP AND STIRS RESTLESSLY. KALI APPEARS AT THE EDGE OF THE STAGE, ADDRESSING AUDIENCE AND KOURETES

KALI:
All night she half-slept,
nauseous, scared, but not quite alone,
listening to movement in her belly

KOURETES:
Staring into the room's huge night
 at her guardian, the hollow-eyed giant

KALI AND KOURETES
called Inanna, with robes like the sky.

LILY [SITTING UP]:
She looks right at me
with eyes that swallow. Hours and hours
of darkness fall into her eyes.

KOURETES:
Inanna, Inanna, Inanna, Inanna
Inanna, Inanna, Inanna, Inanna

KALI:
Then it was morning; she must have slept, finally.

KOURETES:
Dawn pressed hard at her through the trees.
Dawn pressed hard at her through the trees.

LILY [GOING TO THE DOOR]:
I am more nauseous, not even hungry.
SHE PUSHES AT THE DOOR, THEN PACES.

KOURETES:
the door was locked, and the house stayed quiet
all day.

LILY [PACING]:
I don't even think she is there.
Lying down, I knew I would stay there
with the eyes of the centuries on me
longer than a century. All night I half-slept,
nauseous, scared, but not quite alone,
listening to movement in my belly,
reaching constantly with my eyes,
staring into the room's huge night
at my guardian, the hollow-eyed giant
called Inanna, with robes like the sky.

LILY GOES OVER TO LOOK AT THE STATUES

LILY:
so my hunger and sickness kept me . . .

KOURETES:
two more nights, and three more days

LILY:
weak but wakeful. I could see them . . .
In the darkness, she looked right at me
with eyes that swallowed. Hours' and hours'
worth of darkness fell into her eyes.
I could tell it was she, from the bulls' horns
that surmounted her face like the moon,
and the fearless concentration
she stood still with—her towering focus.

KOURETES:
two more nights, and three more days

LILY:
They can see me!
They can see me!

KOURETES:
dozens, watching her with eyes,
squatting goddesses, with children or alone,
alabaster, or dark burned stone,
mouths sometimes open, sometimes in pain,
chipped out hollows shadowing distance,
inset eyes of turquoise staring

KALI:
And the queen of heaven, Inanna,
never left her eyes alone;

LILY [STANDING CENTER STAGE TO FACE AUDIENCE]:
hard on the beams of her eyes I went downward

[SHE FALLS TO THE FLOOR, RAISES HERSELF ON ONE ARM}
till that day passed, and evening came,
and into the second night's solitude

KALI:
there rose another, terrible Queen.
Then it was morning; I guess I'd slept, finally.
Dawn pressed hard at me through the trees.
I was more nauseous, not even hungry,
but I stood up and pushed at the door,
wanting distraction. There were no distractions;
the door was locked, and the house stayed quiet
all day. I don't even think she was there.
So those statues were my companions
two more nights, and three more days,
as my hunger and sickness kept me
weak but wakeful. I could see them,
dozens, watching me with eyes,
squatting goddesses, with children or alone,
alabaster, or dark burned stone,
mouths sometimes open, sometimes in pain,
chipped out hollows shadowing distance,
inset eyes of turquoise staring
from attenuated heights.
And the queen of heaven, Inanna,
never left my eyes alone;
hard on the beams of her eyes I went downward
till that day passed, and evening came,
and into the second night's solitude
there rose another, terrible Queen.

LILY [AS KALI MIMES THE ACTIONS OF THE QUEEN ERESHKIGAL]
She stood over me with the height of a murderer,
her hand on my belly, her voice in my blood,

KALI [AS LILY LIES DOWN]:
Ereshkigel, Ereshkigel

KOURETES:
while Inanna watched without one movement.

LILY [RISING TO HER KNEES]:
Till the dawn came, I felt that hand
burning, and I knew the flame
She stood over me with the height of a murderer,
her hand on my belly, her voice in my blood,
while Inanna watched me without one movement.
Till the dawn came, I felt that hand
burning, and I knew the flame

KALI:
was spinning, heavy, out from her forehead,
resting between my eyes like new wisdom,
as my pregnancy shrank and contracted.
Inanna had taken me to the vision,
and she held me there till it was over,
under Ereshkigal's hand. They all saw me
as death moved through me, and I took a life,
so many of them, without pity or fear,
massed on the shelves with their eyes wide open.

LILY [RISING]:
as death moved through me, and I took a life,
as my pregnancy shrank and contracted.

KOURETES:
as death moved through her, and she took a life
Inanna had taken me to the vision,
and she held me there till it was over,

KALI:
as death moved through her, and she took a life
as my pregnancy shrank and contracted.
Inanna had taken me to the vision,
and she held me there till it was over,
under Ereshkigal's hand. They all saw me
as death moved through me, and I took a life,

so many of them, without pity or fear,
massed on the shelves with their eyes wide open.

KALI AND KOURETES [TO THE TRADITIONAL TUNE]:
Isis, Astarte, Diana, Hecate, Demeter, Kali, Inanna. . .
Death moved through her, and she took a life
Death moved through her, and she took a life

KALI [SLOWLY OPENING THE DOOR AND GOING TO STAND WITH LILY, THEN SPEAKING, NOT SINGING]:
She waited till evening,
with Inanna's eyes on her, steady
as the sun she ruled ruled the day.

KOURETES:
Death moved through her, and she took a life

LILY:
All I wanted was there

KALI AND LILY:
day and its lover, night and its lover

KALI:
brought by Inanna.

LILY:
They healed the pain.

KOURETES:
In the gray light, she left the room.

LILY MOVES OFFSTAGE.

END OF ACT III.

By the third morning, weak and thirsty,
no longer nauseous, I lay in a daze,
waiting for Kali. I waited till evening,
with Inanna's eyes on me, steady
as the sun she ruled ruled the day,
and stopped at dusk. All I wanted was there,
day and its lover, night and its lover,
brought by Inanna. They healed the pain.
In the gray light, I left the room.

Excerpt from ACT III, *Among the Goddesses: An Epic Libretto in Seven Dreams* by Annie Finch (Red Hen Press, 2010).

Everything Intensifies Me
Benedetta Crippa

This painting is a tribute to the divine and the transcendent in every woman, and a reference to the fertile power of the creative act that transforms body and mind. The image can be read as the state of transformation that entrenches Inanna as she experiences the Underworld. I use decoration here as a tribute to human complexity and a form of resistance to aesthetic logics that belittle the feminine. It is also a way to visually research the strange, the inconsequential, and the mysterious. Similarly to the travel of Inanna into the underworld and her ascent from it, I see the creative process as one of destruction, transformation and rebirth.

In order to reach the deepest core of ourselves and allow for radical transformation to happen, we must leave what was imposed on us behind, and initiate ourselves into a process of un-learning. This symbolic, but very tangible death of knowledge paves the way for a process of re-learning, where as newborns, we are receptive of all internal knowledge, and able to bring it into consciousness. We ascend again into the world transformed and gifted of new knowledge, one that we have written from our core.

Inanna: Pregnant with Soul Voice
Iyana Rashil

How does one explain a sudden distaste for domestic cats that occurs out of nowhere? The emotion made no sense at all. I had loved cats all of my life and held no aversion toward any animal. Being a woman who looks for meaning in synchronicities, my curiosity rapidly piqued. What was I dealing with that would have such an unexpected side-effect as to how I felt about my feline friends? With no immediate answers, I set the phenomena aside until reading the shadow aspect of the Moon Card in the Tarot system, where it was revealed that my repugnance was due to a need for me to visit the dark side of the moon in Ereshkigal's realm.[30] This was the design of my invitation into the Dark Queen's domain as Inanna. I was impressed by its mystical presentation.

Unlike common Inanna and Ereshkigal myths, I didn't choose to visit the Dark Queen. Ereshkigal wasn't my patron goddess. I had no altars for her or Inanna. Why wasn't I going to visit Ereshkigal as a descent like other Inanna queens? The only thing I could initially recall for explanation was a ceremony performed for opening the Northern quarter when I was seeking advice of the Dark Mother. Then I remembered an older experience. Years prior, in a meditation, a group of us were guided down an elevator, through a doorway, up a path past a woman and a man, to a pyramid. We were later told that several experiences on this walk had meaning, such as what type of door and garden we walked through, what color hair the woman had, what did the man say? Lastly was the pyramid where most people saw ancient Egyptian artifacts. I did not. I saw tunnel holes stacked to the top of the pyramid. This memory returned to the surface because the Shadow Tarot mentions that the cards were developed with the

---

30 Linda Falorio, *The Shadow Tarot: Dancing with Demons* (1995).
    <http://www.shadowtarot.net/sht29.asp>

Tunnels of Set in mind. There I stood, an Inanna type in Ereshkigal's realm—but I went in through a dark moon tunnel, not the 7 gateways.

The experiences to follow coincided with advanced interpretations of the myth concerning integration of shadow and light, above and below, consciousness and unconsciousness, all aimed at a quest for wholeness. While my experience contained all of the above, it also included the discovery of a treasure in-between those opposites, an experience I haven't found written about. My wholeness was pregnant with soul voice.

It was easy for me to see Inanna's heavenly story before recognizing Ereshkigal's aspects. The heavens had been good to me from a natural mystic, Old Testament, Nazarene and Essene perspective. Terms like Queen and Empress easily rolled off my tongue and were titles clearly understood in soul regards. A soul queen or empress was seen as a woman filled with presence and unassuming in nature. To this end, my visit with Ereshkigal became a royal soul quest rather than suffering a fall, as some tales tell. In my experience, Inanna's Queen-to-Queen encounter with her sister, and wisdom residing in the middle, stimulated new consciousness impregnation.

After the recognition that the integration of opposites and the quest for wholeness included my soul voice pregnancy within, I have repeatedly asked myself a gnawing question, why is it that many who successfully integrate wholeness consciousness, do not as often experience the pregnancy and birth of authentic soul voice and a new regality to their inner queen? Why aren't accomplished wholeness sojourners speaking from their authentic soul nature instead of continuing to recite old male-based interpretations rather than new ones? As I write this I remember a similar question once contemplated: Why do most people pray to Christ hanging on a cross when it is said he is within? In comparison, we can take a moment to see the older Sumerian story of Inanna being dead and hanging on a peg to rise again, and the masculine derived one of Christ. She dies and rises again, and returns to the above. Christ does the same but is also said to have attained keys in his journey to hell. Why wasn't Inanna's story told in this way? With this additional allegory, queens could expect a gathering of keys or gifts on such a journey.

We can now ask what keys did Inanna acquire and why aren't we told? What keys are not mentioned in the male-based interpretations? Have you acquired hidden keys, untold of? In my experience, queens of wholeness can experience an impregnation of new consciousness. If Christ consciousness was born when he rose, why are we missing that a risen Queen's consciousness exists and what type of consciousness is this? Why do we consider this myth to predominantly mean healing? Where is the hidden treasure in the myth?

In part, one piece of treasure is in her sacrifice of Dumuzi and his sister. This key can begin a new chapter in Inanna's story of her ascent. In my experience, the sacrifice of her husband and his sister is the sacrifice of dualistic and patriarchal thinking in favor of a new reign of consciousness. Dumuzi as husband represents a patriarchal controlled thinking via his position as husband, a husband who did not mourn his wife's disappearance or death. He arrogantly sat on her throne, not offering help. Inanna gives this perspective over to Ereshkigal. Dumuzi's sister, also given over to Ereshgikal, represents all woman who agree and protect this dualistic patriarchal mindset of men, which tells women to stay in the place of goddess as consort to the gods or, queens submitted to kings. The sacrifice of these two types of consciousness allowed Inanna to rise again.

The next key we are looking for is that she was escorted out of Ereshkigal's realm to her own queendom without mention of any improvement or treasure of inner voice which brings a new consciousness perspective to the world. Nor are we given interpretation for the in-between from where this new consciousness comes. In interpretation, she only received what she already had previous to her visit in the Underworld. No myth tells us of a death and rebirth without powerful transformation.

I, as Inanna, have lived this recognition for years now after visiting my sister Ereshkigal via a dark moon tunnel. Dualistic old thinking can be sacrificed, in exchange for new queen consciousness from the in-between. This view of the story brings about Inanna as Venus, the morning and evening star in-between night and day. In-between the light and dark side of the moon we can also step into the sphere of pregnant wholeness. Imagine wisdom chromosomes of the above and wisdom chromosomes of the below uniting to give birth to new wisdom from the in-between.

Inanna, as a risen new thinker and ruler, is a story rarely told. What did she do after regaining her throne? Legend suggests that Inanna's name changed to Ishtar, a queen whose reign did not depend on a male consort.[31] Inanna as Ishtar became a queen in rule of her own queendom, whole and greater than before.

Compare this new Inanna/Ishtar to the queen bee who gets pregnant once but for many years births one egg a minute making millions of bees. In us this would be an impregnation of new consciousness where new thoughts and new ideas continually come to birth. We become eternally pregnant with new consciousness, not just whole.

Barren wholeness is 'his story'—so he can discredit the female womb and mind which also conceives to maintain his position as more powerful. Man may have muscles, but an eternally pregnant queen who gestates consciousness is who brings vision in order that humanity doesn't perish. New consciousness birthing after wholeness integration keeps our species alive and thriving while

---

31 *New World Encyclopedia*, Ishtar.
    <http:/www.newworldencyclopedia.org/entry/Ishtar>

man continues to enforce half-thinking—his. A transcended, forever pregnant queen of new consciousness becomes a visionary. As it is said that life without bees would mean humans would die in 4 years, it is also said that without vision, humans will perish. Isn't a fully integrated queen a forward thinking creative ruler in every sense of the word?

It is my feeling that male doctrines and viewpoints should not be forced upon women when they are about the rational mind's submission to silence, rather than wholeness integration and pregnant newness. Even Ereshkigal has been defined improperly by male mentality. Ereshkigal is the reflection Inanna needed to find the middle where the keys are hidden. Women are denied this story in favor of how Ereshkigal is less than—unconscious, demonic, repulsed and unacknowledged—telling us we are damaged goods rather than royal queens on a mission. Ereshkigal remains culturally repressed when in actuality she is a tremendous source of vital power.[32] Is she not a QUEEN doing her task of revealing the middle to daring sisters who would venture into her realm of 'under-standing' seeking their new birth?

We queens can arise as more powerful women—beyond healed or integrated wholeness—by adding this addition to the story of transcending old consciousness. Heaven consciousness abandoned us in our time of greatest need, telling us we stepped out of our place by the Heavenly gods. Only Enki, the God of Wisdom, not a sky god, had compassion and knew the nature of the feminine journey and that Inanna was a vital aspect to all lands and had to be helped.[33]

Men have created many stories to shun this rise of the feminine voice and vision. Most queens rise only to find themselves in

---

[32] Linda Falorio, *The Shadow Tarot: Dancing with Demons* (1995). <http://www.shadowtarot.net>
[33] Diane Wolkstein and Samuel Noah Kramer. *Inanna: Queen of Heaven and Earth* (Harper & Row, Publishers 1983, p. 156)

similar circumstances as before, where men still rule, oppress and direct consciousness through misinterpreting female myths. A true king knows he is less than the inner wisdom of his queen. The 5 book series on Rameses concerning how he treated Nefertiti, is a great reveal in this regard.

It is said that the underworld's journey produces shamans, great magicians and messengers of a new worldview in those who return from it.[34] Yet, no tale tells us of the wisdom of the in-between and how it impregnates new consciousness, not barren wholeness. This accomplishment is easy to recognize. Deeper understandings and mysterious evolutionary views arise from within us, sending wisdom even to our own ears. If you have experienced this, you know.

In Sumerian, the word for ear and wisdom are the same, and, as the ear takes sounds and makes it audible, the wisdom within the core self similarly becomes perceptible.[35] The missing piece is that the wisdom which arises resides where two sides merge to give birth to something new, such as how man and woman can create a child. When this riddle of duality is solved in how we think, authenticity and inner voice can be born. This occurs when leaving a previous version of self behind due to a new way of seeing. Instead of seeing warring opposites and recovering from the scars of finding out that truth was only a half-truth, the inner crowning glory and inner voice of each queen can arise. It is this power of recognition that helps a queen move forward. With her new inner crowning glory, new wisdom and new voice to prosper her queendom with wise leadership, she can find a new reign, whether as a mother, a lover, a spiritual mentor, doctor, political leader or other. This is the rise of a profound inner intelligence, not of the head, not of the gut feel, not of above or below. It is an inner ear awakened at the place in-between in the queen's core court of *Knowings*.

---

34 Ibid., p. 156.
35 Ibid., p. 156.

These gifts of 'understanding' which the journey into unconsciousness bestowed upon me—even though it also took away—kept me content while moving in its dark depths. My creativity increased and I began receiving evolutionary understanding from an eclipse of consciousness which brings a new level of change, where light and dark reverse before becoming whole.[36] In the black mirror of self or the black diamond's many facets, reflections of transformative treasures appeared.

Only by looking back in honest retrospect can I tell you that the years of aching silence I encountered in the dark, led to hearing what would have never been heard if not for my journey into an Inanna type of soul nakedness through the dark moon tunnel. When I stepped again into the light, new insights had been born and my voice had attained to a soul wisdom I had never learned in books. I had reaped an inner prosperity—the ability to hear the wisdom of the in-between. I've succeeded in understanding my own journey and how my new consciousness and voice were born.

The small variances in interpretations of the Inanna and Ereshkigal myth were extremely valuable for me. I discovered later how Ereshkigal willing Inanna's death represented a death to old consciousness in favor of seeing new perspectives which would only arise in this journey through the seven gates, seven in Akkadian meaning wholeness.[37]

Many of you have probably heard the voice of the *Knowings* which comes from within that could not be explained in the past. We can now explain this inner place of queen consciousness which contains our soul voice with Inanna's myth and come to know it more intimately. By taking a look at the word 'understanding' as in

---

36 Crystal Links, Black Sun, <http://www.crystalinks.com/blacksun.html>
37 Diane Wolkstein and Samuel Noah Kramer. *Inanna: Queen of Heaven and Earth* (Harper & Row, Publishers 1983, p. 158)

seeing under where we stood in the old values and beliefs in our mind, we can discover how to look beneath the mind and, in turn, above the unconsciousness represented by Ereshkigal. This center, not Heaven and not the Underworld, between above and below revealed core consciousness which is the profound hidden wisdom positioned on the map by Enki guarding and protecting our true feminine power—the union of the two sisters being two sides of our self. It also reveals how that which we thought in our minds and that which lay dormant in our unconsciousness were only opposite sides of the whole awaiting a profound reunion.

As myths can take on unique meanings for each of us, what came to matter most to me is that all queens can rise again refreshed and whole after entering the great below of Ereskigal. After seeing the underworld of self and finding out the deceptions in the world above, they can redress their consciousness and soul in an even finer regalia of royalty then before they entered their unconscious and faced the inner pain, becoming whole in countenance without the need for false patriarchal supports any longer because the in-between, where soul voice resides, was discovered.

Hail to the Inanna in all women! Who else can accomplish such a beautiful goal to give birth to the story only the inner soul voice can tell!

I Wear the Sun and Moon on my Crown
Sinem Alev Koca

Upon day-spring, the forest spirits bade me farewell.
Their work was done—guarding my shivelighted slumber,
they allowed but the birds to awaken their maiden,
and the prancing birds belted out their ode to summer.

I opened my fresh eyes, lain amidst a bed of dew—
lain amidst a cheering choir, greeted by ancient rite—
Is this my mother's embrace? Have I now her face?
Have I swallowed her wisdom by travelling the night?

World! I am a woman in my luminous fullness,
yet never so feminine as when I came to finish
the annals of martyrdom and scribe the new chapter
of laughing storms and gracious beginnings.

Pomegranate and hibiscus, basil and lotus—
The fragrances gold-spun into your darkest dreams.
I weave the shadows into the kilim of my life—
Sage and sentinel, they embellish my carpet's seams.

World! I am Inanna the Lion, rose-cheeked and strong;
And awesome Ereshkigal, retribution and squall.
Mine are the march of spring—the hope—the hearts;
Mine are the war cry—the torch—the robe of stars!

Hear me out!—I say—I am Inanna!
Prime mover and glory and light and song!
Hear me out!—I say—I am the Lion!
Mine are the throne of Heaven!
The darkness! The lessons!

Daphne's Descent

Daphne Moon

I'd like to say that my descent (and subsequent ascent), like Inanna's, was one trip down deep and back out. But it seems my life was more a series of dives, deeper and deeper, small ascents, and further dives, until I started my final climb a few years ago. But to understand it all, we have to start at the beginning.

I was born Rachael Nicole Patterson on Oct. 15, 1987 to Dick and Terry Patterson. I am a Libra with a Cancer moon and a Virgo rising —as a result, I feel deeply, desire balance on the inside and come across to most as a highly organized perfectionist. Because of these conflicting ways of being, I began struggling with depression and anxiety at a very young age. Even photos of me at 3 show a deep sadness in my eyes. My parents moved me and my little brother out to a small town in East Texas when I was going into 1st grade, as a way to protect us from the violence and drugs of the city. My father had just found Jesus and was determined to do a better job raising us than his alcoholic parents had done with him.

What we found was a school with excellent scores and a strong tradition of corporal punishment. It wasn't until 5th grade that the state passed a law that required parental permission to give out licks, and the rule in my house was licks at school meant licks at home (even once that did pass, they signed the paperwork to let them hit us whenever they wanted). Dad was careful to sit us down and tell us about how much more it hurt him than it did us, how we had brought this on ourselves, but that we could choose —over the bed, or over his lap. Hand or belt. How generous he was to allow us to play pick-your-abuse.

The worst, though, was around my birthday when I was 17. The previous spring I'd been told I needed to be back from curfew an hour early because of daylight savings time. I inquired as to whether that meant in the fall I'd get an extra hour. I was told yes, and clung tight to that memory. When the fall finally rolled around I had some friends over for board games and around 11:30 we decided to go for ice cream at the local diner. My father marched outside and asked where I was going. I explained and he said I didn't have time because of curfew. I reminded him of the conversation from the spring and he denied it happening. Told me I had 30 minutes to be back inside and left. Being the rebellious, angry teen I was (but being crazy afraid of him) I didn't leave but I did walk to the end of the driveway to smoke a cigarette. He came barreling out of the house and grabbed my arm, dragging me inside in front of all my friends. I was screaming and they were terrified. They quickly left as he pulled me in the house and proceeded to berate me. I stepped back each time he stepped toward me and when my back was against the wall he raised his hand and I yelled, "Don't fucking touch me!"

He squatted down and started chanting this thing my little brother used to annoy me, "I'm not touching you, I'm not touching you" while waving his fingers in my face.

I slow clapped. "Good job Dad. Teach me to be an adult by acting like an 8-year-old."

The rest is pretty fuzzy. I remember being thrown into the bar chairs, onto the ground. I remember him on top of me, my arms over my face, him hitting me over and over. I remember my mom coming in and making him stop, but comforting and consoling him while he cried, and sending me to my room.

So, what happens when you put a kid who already tends toward depression and anxiety into a home where the parents are emotionally and physically abusive?

You get self-destruction.

Alcoholism was strong in my family, they said. I should be careful with my consumption. It was like playing with fire. They never talked about the cause of the alcoholism—the need to escape the deep, dark hell that is depression. The inability to get out of bed. The lack of desire to sleep that was quickly replaced with sleeping for days. The ravenous hunger that turned into revulsion at the sight of food. The spiraling thoughts of guilt and shame and self-hatred that would drive even the sanest person in the world to cutting themselves or drinking to drown the desire to do so.

And let me tell you, I was a perfectionist at self-destruction. I was talented at personal manipulation, convincing myself it was fine. I was fine. This is just how things were. It was better than being who they wanted me to be.

I was in my first abusive romantic relationship at 15. He forced me to look at porn and when I told him I wasn't really sure I was ready to have sex, he told me it didn't matter. I rarely ever tried to say no after that, to anyone. It was just easier to do it than have someone tell me it didn't matter if I wanted to or not. Plus I got pretty good at convincing myself I did want it, always. When I was 18 I had a boyfriend who was 10 years older than me that would pick me up by my throat and slam me against the wall. He was a veteran, it wasn't his fault, I'd say. Meanwhile I drank and drank more.

Then two days before my 19th birthday, I'm driving home from Austin to Canton through deep East Texas on a back highway that's rarely used and sparsely populated. I looked into the floor for my CD case and when I looked up an 18-wheeler was making its way into my lane. I was terrified and swerved, and about 2/3 of the way through the spin into the median I realized I had lost control. Then I heard my uncle's voice, "If you lose control, let go. Relax. Surrender. Drunk drivers survive because they don't brace for impact. Sober people try to regain control, and they die."

So, I let the wheel go, looked at the ceiling, and said, "OK God, if I see you, I see you."

Immediately, the side of my car hit the dirt wall and I blacked out. Next thing I know there's a crowd of people and an ambulance. I'm sitting on the ground and some woman is holding my hand and I'm crying, then I see the care flight land. I jump up, frantic, asking if I'd killed someone. "My mother will kill me, please did I hurt someone?"

Even in the most traumatic moment of my life, I still blamed myself. I was still afraid of what my family would do.

It took the paramedic grabbing my shoulders and saying, "That's for you. Please sit down. We think you may have broken your neck." To pull me out and get me to look at myself. My clothes were torn, I was covered in blood. My hands were covered in blood. It was dripping off my brow. I sat down and let them take care of me. I called my parents over and over, then my boyfriend, then my best friend. Then they gave me morphine and I passed out.

I woke up in the hospital to the orthodontist grabbing either side of my jaw, wiggling them in opposite directions, and saying they'd schedule me to have it wired shut. They struggled to take off my piercings for the MRI. Then I don't remember anything until the morning.

I woke up to a man standing over me. It took me a second to register what was happening. There was an IV in each of my arms. This man was black and in his 50s or 60s at least, wearing his boxers and a button-down shirt that was open in the front. One hand was on my breast and the other was holding his genitals. He was mumbling about how much I liked it. Luckily I was able to get nurses in to pull him off of me before he'd actually managed to figure out how to penetrate me, though it was quite close.

My parents had gone for breakfast. The man was a dementia patient, he'd escaped the psych ward, gone down an elevator, passed a nurse's station and came into my room undetected. The police asked if I wanted to file a report. My mother said it wasn't his fault, he was sick, that I shouldn't press charges. I couldn't sue the hospital if I didn't press charges, but I wanted it to be over, and I listened to my mom.

The self-destruction got worse. Plus, my body was broken, and I didn't have my old outlets—dance, running, they told me I'd never do either again. That I'd be on pain meds for the rest of my life. A friend at work suggested yoga. I tried it off and on throughout the years and it always helped but I was also always struggling financially because of my alcohol dependency so I never took it seriously. Eventually, 5 1/2 years later, I hit rock bottom.

I was living in a one-bedroom apartment with 5 other people, occasionally prostituting myself for drugs and a little cash. My parents offered to let me move home, and I resisted at first but eventually relented. When you realize you've lost control, let go, surrender. I'd do the thing I said I'd never do and drop the wheel. The literal next day I walked into a coffee shop that I didn't know existed and saw a flyer for a yoga studio that had opened in that town right around the same time I'd moved away. There was a card for a free class, and I took it. I showed up and, unbeknownst to me, walked into a class with the owner of the studio. I loved it; when I stayed after to talk to her she called me a yogi and handed me a flyer for a teacher training program. I left crying. Over the next six months I dove into that program. She put me on a payment plan and I worked a little just to afford to pay for it. I rehabilitated my body and my mind, became stronger and more flexible than I'd known possible. This was the beginning of my ascent out of the hole into which I'd dug.

Now, I'm sure it'd be lovely to hear that I never had a tough thing happen again. But that's not how life works. I still struggled with relationships and alcohol consumption and self-destruction but I had a bit of a safety net now. I didn't seem to dip as low, I was able to pull myself up and out most days. I could pay my rent, plus feed myself. It was an accomplishment.

Then, in 2014, I got pregnant.

I didn't intend to be a mother. As a matter of fact, I adamantly swore I'd never do it.

But I tried and tried to make the call to get an appointment at the clinic and I always broke into tears. Eventually, I decided I was gonna be a mom. I told my boyfriend and he was supportive. He'd always been very in love with me and I was always kind of distant. I was afraid to try to do this alone and he thought it was how he was going to make sure I never left. Pregnancy was amazing; he was always so supportive and helpful. I got my natural birth and he was my birth coach. I thought we were going to be the perfect partners.

I was wrong. It didn't take long for him to develop the same abusive habits I'd seen before. I turned into a terrified mouse of a woman, focused on keeping my son safe from his rages. One night I was fed up and tried to leave. He threw me across the room, prevented me from leaving, threw my phone into a fish tank and broke it, choked me, and didn't stop until one of his friends intervened.

He went to jail, and I called my parents and they came, even though it was 3 in the morning. The next day, my dad said he'd talk to him and make sure he understood that what happened wasn't OK. I gave him cash out of the savings to bail him out of jail. He came home full of apologies and promises. I believed him, but it didn't take long for things to go back to his normal. I took a second teacher training in the spring of 2016. By the end of it, I knew I needed to leave. I packed my things while he was at work one day with the help of a friend and left him a note. I stayed away from him for a few days, but because I felt guilty for keeping our son from him, I started going back over there. He'd feed me, give me money, beg me to come home. It didn't take long for me to go back. A few weeks tops. But it also didn't take long for me to realize what was happening, and plan to leave more permanently.

It took a while, but I found my way. I was transient for about 6 months but moved into my apartment in March of 2017. My therapy through Genesis Women's Shelter has been instrumental in my healing, along with a new healing modality—ecstatic dance. I dance and I practice yoga and I travel with a healing space called the Goddesses of Light Temple. I hold ceremonies for survivors of domestic and sexual violence, offering each woman a chance to be heard. Because we heal when we share our stories and are received without judgment or someone trying to fix us.

I accepted Spirit's call to let go of my old name and step into my new one, Daphne Moon, in July of 2017. I'd been using it in ceremony and it was clear that it was time to accept that the old me had died and a new me had risen from the ashes. I'd stripped down my old beliefs about what made me strong and discovered a significantly more powerful version of myself. Then I hung on stakes of my own making until I felt like my flesh was rotting, until I realized that I alone had the power to walk away.

Seshat's Portal
Patricia Ballentine

A Journey with Inanna

Glenys Livingstone Ph.D.

Forty years ago (1978) I signed a letter to an editor "in the name of She who is rising;" he had rejected an article I had submitted on women and religion. Indeed, many now witness that She has risen since then, prolifically, and ever more so, collectively; and also for me personally. I reflect on those forty years as they unfolded personally: It has been a terrible journey. It may sound surprising to say that the journey has been "terrible" when the outcome in my life in more recent times has been so fruitful, creative and beautiful. But it did indeed require a descent—an initiation, for which I largely thank the power of Inanna. Inanna knows about descent and stripping back, cleaning up. She may answer your call for Her integrity—for Her wholeness—with an obliging journey to the Underworld, a visit to the Great Below, the realm of Her sister Ereshkigal. In an earlier reflection on the journey, I stated:

> *I was fortunate, my life did fall apart, I was lost. The journey into Her story, means a participation in Her descent and return, it means a shattering of what went before. How does a woman stop being object, and become subject? How does she become the body in her own mind? It requires more than a headtrip, it requires the descent of Inanna, a falling apart. I was still a product of patriarchal narrative, and still seeking the Beloved (the Mother) outside myself. What did it take to move from that, to allow a fertile darkness within, from which the Self could begin? The regaining of integrity, and an understanding of why we lost it, or did not have it, can require a great darkness.*[38]

---

38 Glenys Livingstone, *PaGaian Cosmology*, p.76.

Sometimes one's deepest desires require a journey one would not have the stomach for: Her shattering is merciful. The mystics of many religious traditions have sung of the beauty of the dark night —"more lovely than the dawn" as John of the Cross expressed it, and dark Goddesses have been revered for their awesome and creative dismantling. Chamunda, a skeletal Deity of India for example, has been praised with: "only terrifying to those who oppose Her, for Her devotees She is a powerful vigilant guardian. Chamunda belongs to the group of 'matrikas'—the powerful Mothers who ensure universal order."[39] Inanna's power is in Her daring to descend, to get to the bottom of things, to subject Herself to the truth, to trust that She will return—and Her trust is also in the faithfulness and resourcefulness of the companion Ninshubur who will wait for Her at the entrance, who will send for help if she senses its need. Inanna's power is in Her fierce passion for life and beauty, and Her journey is one of true heraics,[40] calling forth the power in one's depths—and the shared desires of companions, watchful attentive others.

The portal for me into the journey with Inanna was a ritual weekend workshop with a group of women, facilitated by a skilled woman, in 1991. We joined Inanna in a ritual descent, giving over personal representations of what was requested at each of the seven gates to the Great Below. I knew something was not right in my life, though I did not know what or why—but I knew I desired deeply to set it right, and I was willing to give myself over to this Goddess, to strip myself back with Inanna; to allow only Her grace in any re-emergence. I deeply wanted Her garden in my soul, not the weeds that seemed to be strangling me. So in the process of the Inanna ritual, I gave up significant real things at each of the

---

39 Adele Getty, *Goddess: Mother of Living Nature*, p.84
40 This term is based on Charlene Spretnak's advice that "hera" (a pre-Hellenic word for Goddess) predates "hero", a term for the brave male Heracles who carries out the bidding of his Goddess Hera. Charlene Spretnak notes that the derivative "heroine" is completely unnecessary. See "Mythic Heras as Models of Strength and Wisdom", in *The Politics of Women's Spirituality*, p.87.

seven gates, as Inanna does. I cannot remember them all exactly, but there were my keys (to house and car and all) left at one of the gates, and my jewellery was left at another. I took off significant clothing at another gate. I left significant books that represented my intellect and learning. Each participant left what she was willing to give at each gate, not knowing if or how that capacity or power would be restored. Not every woman was as radical as I was willing to be; She meets each where they are it seems. She listens to the heart and each one's yearnings. Mine were earnest and deep: I wanted Her. We slept that night in a room together in the Underworld we had descended to, to join Inanna as a "rotten piece of meat" in the realm of Ereshkigal.

Within the year, my life fell apart and I was shattered: The image I had at that time about my situation was of a rocket that had gone straight up and turned back to Earth, crashing like broken glass into millions of pieces. The poison was exposed. Here is a poem I wrote within the next few years that ensued, as I reflected on what had taken place:

Transformation

Completely dismantled
—all the stock taken out of the cupboards.
Strip them bare
Pull apart my knowings
—rip them open, let the connections be severed.

Expose all the parts, every cell
to the sunlight
de-toxify
throw away
move it all around
mix it, mix it
skim the dross

With mortar and pestle pound Her
Is She mortified sufficiently yet?
Has She seen it all yet?
Pound Her more, take it from Her

Like panning for gold...
    is there any?
What will be left?

The grit, the metal, the stones
    found at the bottom of the wash
This is the new composition.
Begin composing it now.

Write it, sing it, melt it back together,
    re-Form it, re-Cognize it,
    breath it, dance it.

Let it grow

Praise the Dark One who dismantled you dear
    who took off your robes
    exposed you

She took you apart
—because you lusted to know
Now She has filled your cells,
    your blueprint
        with new possibility
—bled the poison
    emptied the cup
        that it may be filled.

I wrote many things at that time: The dark is a fertile place. I asked many questions, re-viewed details of my life as I had been living it —now that truth had been revealed and heretofore hidden shapes and stories could be seen. I was horrified. I was frozen. I was the "rotten piece of meat" as is described in Inanna's story. I wrote: "My passive body washed up onto the shores of a dark island."

There is no doubt that commitment to such a process, to a journey with Inanna, requires daring and courage, and trust in Her; but that will arrive if one is passionate enough to know truth and integrity. I did return, along with those who had been harmed in the midst of my blindness. We have returned, we made it back from the Underworld, to the sweet surface, with the riches of the dark journey. I have been deeply graced, in the reconstruction of myself, an organic re-creation out of Her clay and earth, not of glass—and in the company of others who came, desiring my well-being, the gifts that they saw I held embryonically. My re-emergence was with the assistance of a web of companions, some who came from afar, were unknown before, as well as through the power I discovered within me. It was an emergence into Inanna's garden—the original sacred Garden, a new place for me, where She flourishes and bears fruit for many. The hera's journey with Inanna is to return with the goods, the self-knowledge, a lot wiser and radiant: to be like the Sun and the Moon and the stars, and regenerate the world.

© Glenys Livingstone 2018

References:

Getty, Adele. *Goddess: Mother of Living Nature*. London: Thames and Hudson, 1990.

Livingstone, Glenys. *PaGaian Cosmology: Reinventing Earth-based Goddess Relgion.* NE: iUniverse, 2005.

Spretnak, Charlene (ed). *The Politics of Women's Spirituality*. NY: Doubleday, 1982.

The Magic Pouch
Annelinde Metzner

I have released my magic pouch.
Fathom this—the miracle sac nestled in my abdomen
where spirits come to Earth and find their destiny.
This wondrous space that grows exponentially
to accommodate a new human being!
I have released my uterus!
Here I am to honor you, oh alchemical gift,
carrier of the species, deliverer of DNA.
Oh place of pure regeneration!
Miracle tubes where fertilization occurs;
Ovaries, hatchery of the round perfection of femaleness,
oak-split egg basket where my mother and grandmother
held me tenderly too;
cervix, precious tunnel that, entranced,
widens a thousand times for human birth.
Oh wine-sac, imbued with love,
Oh world gift, numinous as the stars,
womb of all creation,
meeting place of divine spirit and blessed flesh,
welcome center for all our souls.
With this release I honor you, magic sac,
locus of intense and sexual feeling,
dark cave I have loved and honored all these years.
Woman's divine chamber
which we must guard from violation,
our own and our sisters',
which we pray for and protect
throughout our lives.
Sanctuary and cauldron of mind, spirit and flesh.
In letting you go, I hold you up,

I see you now for what you are.
I prostrate myself before you.
Oh womb who has made of me a shaman,
as all women are!
I have offered my body for the incarnation of souls.
If women deem it right and good
for all of us and for ourselves,
we will usher in a life.
Oh magic sac that made me
a conduit of the divine,
I hold you now in my open palm,
acknowledging your perfection,
astonished as, like a butterfly just emerged from its cocoon,
I open my hand and let you go free.

Artist wishes to remain anonymous.
Shared with her permission.

My Own Inanna: A Rebirthing
Rev. DiAnna Ritola

Ah, Goddess! I hurt. My heart. My guts, my back, my shouldersmyheadmyheartmyheartmyheart

This was my litany day after day, morning and evening, waking and sleeping, and parenting my toddlers. For over a year I had been aware of being miserable... though the misery had crept up slowly for a couple years before I was able to acknowledge the severity of my ache.

The heartache of living life in a box of my husband's expectations, my parents' expectations, and what I assumed to be the world's expectations had manifested into real physical pain, and I could no longer deny the source of my low back pain, my headaches, or my difficulty digesting food. I had cut off so much of myself to be the person I was "supposed" to be—while also donning the trappings of the roles I was playing—that I no longer knew who I really was.

I distracted myself from the misery of my marriage by focusing on my children. Beautiful, strong, healthy daughters ages 4 and 2 who relied on me to hold my shit together—to make the food, plan the outings, help them to dress and clean up, change the diaper, feed the dogs, keep the structure of our lives intact. I used daily routine to numb out and keep the mask in place so as not to upset the functioning of the family, yet behind the mask I was withering.

In the prior decade I had found my spiritual connection to the Goddess. I had studied ancient Goddess myths and felt the resonance within that made me feel more alive and at peace and to find joy in my body and the beauty of sex, but this situation was different, or so I thought. I felt too filled with shame to stay in the presence of Her for too long. I hadn't yet realized that She could hold my rage. I wanted to yell and scream and to say cruel words or run away and pretend none of it was real. I felt like I should fix things, or fix me. I wanted my husband to disappear or die so that I wouldn't have to deal with the fact that we had changed, that I had changed. I was angry that I couldn't, and really didn't want to be the wife, mother, and person that I had been raised to be: the person who had entered into that marriage as a heterosexual woman, but who knew that mask, too, was a lie.

As I was walking this road of loneliness and fear, I reached out to a friend. I was telling her how much my soul was hurting... so much so that my body was in pain. And she, wise woman that she was, said "Of course it hurts; you're birthing yourself."

Of course, it hurts. You're birthing your Self.

I stopped complaining and just gaped realizing the depth of TRUTH in those words. The pain suddenly became an ally and not an enemy, just like the pain of laboring to bring my daughters into the world. I realized that in order to birth myself, I had to go deeper than I had ever gone before, into my own center, to find the Self I needed to become.

I knew of Inanna and her journey to her sister, Ereshkigal. I wish I could say that I took comfort in knowing that she got out of it ok, so I probably would, too. But, come on, I'd spent a few years of marriage solidifying the lessons that my parents taught: The man is the head of the household. Marriage, however difficult, is better than being single. Women are supposed to do most of the work in keeping a relationship together. Working women and single mothers cause damage to their children. And, more. Like Inanna, I had layers of hubris to discard.

I also had my own human tendency to avoid dealing with uncomfortable reality. I had spent years stuffing my feelings into a small spot somewhere inside. If I didn't look at them, then they weren't real, right? So why did I keep thinking about these "unreal" feelings?

I wanted something different. I wanted to be happy and content in my life. I wanted to wake up and have everything that was "wrong" in my life and my marriage changed into the way things "should" have been. However, it's pretty difficult to make changes in your life when you're not being honest with yourself.

After many months of asking, prodding, and insisting, my husband agreed to try marriage counseling. Within a couple sessions, the counselor suggested that my husband have a few sessions alone. I, too, was beginning to wake up to my own need for healing, not as a wife, but as a woman.

I was 31 years old. It was time to GET REAL. I found an amazing therapist for myself. Her skills, presence, and wisdom helped me to find a way to begin my descent into my heart. I began to open up in deeper and more profound ways. In order to shed my trappings of the image I had created and grow into a more wholistic version of myself, I had to get really honest about who I was at that point and how I had let myself go into hiding. It took a few months before I started to notice that I was feeling better. I started swimming to help my back, and I became very aware of what foods I was eating. I would see this same therapist off and on for the next 5 years.

I also started to reclaim my connection to the Goddess and my feminine spirit and sexuality through music, meditation, reading inspiring books, and continuing to learn about myself. I finally started to feel like *I* was important enough to listen to. And what my heart was saying was: You are not meant for this marriage; you and your children deserve a better atmosphere at home.

My husband and I separated in early 2004 after 10 years of marriage, and I came out of the closet as a lesbian. Even though I was still working on my "stuff," I was able to reclaim my joy in many areas of my life. I wasn't trying to pretend I was someone else: a copy of my mother, some mythological "perfect" wife, or a straight woman. I determined that in the years ahead I would parent my children differently. I would teach them positive attitudes about their bodies, about love, and about the ups and downs of relationships. Not trying to fit into a box made by someone else allowed me to reclaim those parts of me that I had cut off (or been forced to cut off) in order to fit into the box labeled "Appropriate Woman."

I went back to college (16 years after I started), working toward my Bachelor's Degree. When I finished my degree in December 2008, at the ripe age of 37, I thought about continuing my education to become a sex therapist. But there was a different path for me. In conversation with a friend, she mentioned that she was considering enrolling in a 2-year seminary to become ordained as an Interfatih Minister and to practice as a spiritual counselor. I sensed and felt the hand of the Goddess in this, and I knew that I wanted that, too.

During my 3 years in undergrad, I had continued to shed my old self and talk with others about their journeys and challenges. I noticed recurring themes: things like assumptions, self-esteem, difficulty with sexual conversations and asking for what I wanted, questions about pain and sexual violence, and how much of that created barriers to trusting myself... and others. The more I unpacked and worked on healing these areas, the more frequently I seemed to have conversations with other folks about just these topics. I realized people are hungry to talk about sex and relationships in a non-shaming, exciting, affirming, and, yes, spiritual way.

My children are now young adults and they had all the information on sex and spirituality they could handle (and maybe more than they wanted to hear from their mom!) throughout their childhood. They are the ones their friends turned to in their teen years for accurate information and support. I've created a life filled with joy, yummy sex, and peace with my past. I use the wisdom I have gained to hold the container of enquiry for others to step into their own power in the journey through the Underworld of the Self to learn what is no longer needed to be the person they wish to be.

Each cycle of my life offers me the opportunity to revisit Inanna's Descent through my own journey. In order to continue becoming, I must be willing to let go of my trappings, to stand naked and vulnerable in the light of my own truth, and to face my deepest fears with as much courage as I can muster. When I do so, I realize the deep truth of my own integrity, so that what I think, what I say, and what I do are in alignment with my Goddess Self.

Permission to Fall Apart
Nina Erin Hofmeijer

I grant you permission to fall apart.

here,
I will make you this nest
here,
I will tie your hair back
here,
I will wait with you

Your heart is a stone sunk to the bottom
of the bottom
Hot and cold
a dead thing, pulsating
a thing that cannot be

Let it be that.

Your skin is coming off,
peeling and sloughing around the
coarse string you've used to truss
yourself, to keep your old shape,
the one we all rely on

Cut it off; shed it all

The howl that is developing
in the subterranean pockets
of your grief,
that is swirling behind your name,
a sound that is a mouth in shock at its gaping

Release it
Here. Now.

Look in the mirror of my face
See what I see:
All that you broke was already broken
See what I see:
All that you shed was no longer yours

Your renewal is centuries old,
made of the shed pieces of the
winters of your ancestors

Your storm is the honest expression of the sun:
Turning seeds to crops, turned thresh turned dust

Explosions of stardust and the wind of creation;
We are what's left after God fell apart

Inanna's Ascent: Taking the Tough Love of the Shadow-Sister Back to the Light

Lyn Thurman

I heard the call from the Great Below and I followed into the darkness. I travelled down, deeper and deeper, unware of the challenges ahead and oblivious of the map left by Inanna. I didn't know Her then and I didn't know I was following Her descent. I was lost.

Sometimes we choose to hear the call but oftentimes, we are plunged into chaos then we scramble, in a panic, to make sense of the world around us. Stability crumbles, relationships end, beliefs are questioned and the emptiness we hid within reveals itself. We are challenged, stripped naked and forced to view reality with a new pair of eyes. The descent is far from pretty; it's brutal. Because our modern society ignores our despair or covers up feelings of disconnection with consumerism or contempt, we are unaware that this difficult journey has been traversed before and once we face what we fear or what is broken, we can find freedom.

Inanna makes her journey to the underworld to see her sister, Ereshkigal, the Queen of the Dead. This shadow-sister strips Inanna of her jewellery, her clothes and eventually her life. As the story unfolds, Inanna is resurrected, and the final lines of the epic poem give prais—not to Inanna, the Queen of Heaven, but to Ereshkigal. Without Ereshkigal forcing her sister to reveal her nakedness and vulnerability, Inanna could not become whole.

My descent happened when I was in my late twenties. My life fell apart in a short space of time. My husband had an affair then left me to raise our two infant sons alone. Changes in my government job coincided with my divorce and I was moved into a new department with a boss who resented me for turning down the promotion he offered. My relationship with my parents disintegrated through disagreements on how I should raise my sons. I was uninvited to my brother's wedding. My best friend found Jesus as she settled into married life while I had neither to cling to. Eventually, the labels I'd worn for my adult life did not apply: I was no longer a wife, daughter, sister, best friend or employee. I'd been stripped of all I knew, and I faced the darkness without knowing if I'd ever see the light again. I rested there for a while, letting depression overwhelm me.

My lowest point was deciding my sons could do much better without me. Their father and my parents were eager to grab them, and what could I offer my sons? I didn't know who I was apart from broken and empty. One Sunday afternoon while they were visiting their father, I wrote each a note, so they could understand how much I loved them and why I couldn't go on any longer.

My suicide was the kindest option for them, I believed. But before I could act on my decision, my old, yellow Labrador nudged me as I was curled up on the sofa then he waited for a walk. One final walk wouldn't make much difference in my plans, so I found the leash and headed uphill to the woods. As I wandered half-heartedly through the trees, I looked up at the clouds and a sliver of hope pierced my soul.

Life was, at least on the outside, pretty good before my descent. However, if you had been privy to peer at my soul you would have seen a different reality. I wasn't well-suited to my husband and we had very little in common, apart from our sons and a history that went back to nursery school. I was deeply unhappy at work in a job I had taken as a teenager because I felt pressured to earn money and become a responsible adult. My parents believed support came through control, and you either complied or were iced out of their lives. I ate to dull my emotional pain and subjected my body to bouts of overeating followed by starvation —I could not remember a time since I was 15 that I wasn't on a diet.

The thing about a descent into the underworld is that amongst the deepest and darkest depression and the chaos of a life falling around your ears, you find clarity. It's the gift of your shadow-sister, your inner Ereshkigal, who has lured you into this space for you to see life for what it really has become. She shows you who you are becoming. If I'd known about Inanna's descent back them, I would have realised that the stripping away of my identity and security were part of a process and through this difficult, challenging time I would find wholeness.

The sudden absence of the traditional masculine roles of husband, father and boss made me realise that I didn't need them. They were all figures that had assisted in collapsing my world and I knew I didn't need them to build my life back up. The clarity I found in the darkness helped give me strength to trust in myself. I won't pretend that it was easy because it wasn't. I grieved hard over these men, like Ereshkigal did for her dead husband, but also like Her, I was labouring a new life. I was in pain but something new was about to emerge from the dark journey I had found myself on.

After my husband left, I felt free to bring down books I had hidden away in the attic. Since I was a little girl, I had an interest in the mysteries of life, the occult and spirituality. This first went against my parents' beliefs and then my ex-husband's. Rather than be strong to who I was, I hid my interests to appear 'normal' like everyone else. Once there were no longer risks of being called a weirdo or freak, I was free to explore what spirituality meant to me. I found meaning, connection and a path that felt as if I were coming home. I walk the same path today as a witch.

Reconnecting with my spiritual core gave me a centre from which to rebuild my life. My first decision was not to settle into a relationship with anyone who did not share similar beliefs to my own. I realised I would prefer to be alone than to be in a superficial relationship. As I found myself on a less than traditional path, I realised I might have to wait some time to find a good fit. As it turns out, my wait-time wasn't very long at all and exactly a year to the day that my divorce was final, I married again to a man who has been my companion and spiritual co-adventurer for over fifteen years now.

The ascent from Ereshkigal's darkness into Inanna's world of light is not without its tests. You don't take the journey to meet your inner Ereshkigal and come out unchanged. You gain a deeper understanding about what it means to be you and what values you hold. You see your truth in Ereshkigal and then you must be courageous to live it when you emerge. And the tests will come. Will you revert to your old ways because it's less painful or will you find the strength to be true to your very essence? I lost blood-family relationships because I could not betray my own truth. When other people are not willing to love you for who you are then you have no choice but to let them go. If you hold on because they provide familiarity, you block new relationships from growing in the void. Even Inanna, the queen of heaven, no longer had the same relationship with her lover Dumuzid after she returned from the underworld. The descent changes you, and you carry the marks of change as you walk your ascent with Inanna.

Taking Inanna's descent—then returning from it—isn't solely about relationships. The journey shakes the foundations of everything around you and if you had built a life that wasn't in alignment with your truth then it will crumble. Usually, this blessing requires the dust to settle before you can see the gifts you've been given. Without the implosion of Inanna's descent, how many of us would still be in unsatisfactory jobs or unfulfilling spiritual practice? We settle and wait for something better to happen to us and invariably, it does not and yet we still wait. We need the hard love of a cosmic big sister to shake us awake and compel us to strive for better. We take control back even if it is with weak knees and an anxious heart at first.

While in the middle of my own personal chaos, I knew I could not go back to the hostile work environment at my government job. I had watched my manager play politics and work around policies to make two women redundant. I was next on his list. The stress and tension made me physically ill and I dreaded going to the office. It was out of alignment with who I was becoming and while the regular pay was nice, it was no longer enough to keep me tethered to a place I had grown to despise. I quit and breathed a sigh of relief. I wasn't brave enough yet to leave the security of paid employment behind, so I found another job and stayed there for a couple of years, using the time to gain more experience and to start my own little side hustle business. Eventually, I took the leap into full time self-employment because I knew I'd never be truly happy in a 'traditional' workplace environment.

Without experiencing my own descent, I doubt I would have found the courage to become self-employed. My working-class family stuck to corporations and nine-to-five work weeks to make a living. When your whole world is shaken and stirred, you see the world with clarity. Illusions fall away. Inherited beliefs demand questioning and you can free yourself from self-imposed chains. Of course, self-employment hasn't been without its challenges, but I've built a working lifestyle that fits around me rather than me having to fit around it. I work from home so I can be with my family and home-school my daughter. Importantly for me, my work is not confined to one activity. I use my IT, design and office skills to help other small businesses navigate the online world. But I also fulfil the role of priestess by mentoring and teaching others.

One of the benefits that has come from shrugging off the corporate world has been creativity. Before Inanna and I walked down the dark path to see Ereshkigal, I didn't believe in my creativity (although I did as a child). Emerging from the darkness puts life in perspective and you realise that you too hold the divine feminine gift of creativity. You must create for yourself because who else is going to rebuild your life after it has fallen to your feet? If you give away your power, someone else will create your life in the way he sees fit. Creativity trickles down into all areas of life once you remove the blocks that were stopping it from manifesting. I am creative in my work and I now find enjoyment in creativity where once all I found was frustration. I write, I cook, I make art.

My life would look very different today if I had not heard the call of the Great Below and faced the darkness. Of course, my life would have also been a lot shorter had I not taken my dog for a final walk and felt hope return to me. Coming up the descent has given me far more gifts and blessings than I would ever have imagined. I found my truth and I live it. I am a happier, stronger woman after finding Inanna and Ereshkigal in the darkest night of my soul.

Reiki
Melissa Stratton Pandina

Intention of Truth: My Journey Through the Underworld with the Dark Goddess

Sacred Storytelling by Genevieve Deven

Introduction:

On a crisp January afternoon, standing in sacred space with my soul-sisters, I voiced an intention aloud —"to live in truth." I was naïve at how impactful those words would become. The Goddess heard my intent and quickly came to call, revealing painful, life-altering truths. In that swirling vortex of tribulation, the Dark Goddess asked me to dance and I was finally ready to say yes. I am forever changed and forever grateful to our Dark Mother for her transformative journey through the dark and back into light. This is my homage to Her and Her journey through the underworld:

Invocation:

Inanna, great mother, lost in the underworld, can you be found?
Kali, dark mother, destroyer of ego, burn it all down.
Pele, she who spits fire, the fire of destruction and creation.
Medusa, violated maiden, it wasn't her fault, victim no more.
Erishkigal, queen of the underworld, goddess of forgiveness and release.
Hecate, I've come to your crossroads, triple goddess, goddess of magic.
Persephone, you found your power and a new life in the underworld.
Queens of the dark, queens of the dead, queens of the night –
The dark night of the soul.
....

My Sacred Story:

I'm walking along in love and light.
There's so much joy in all the little things, at least for me.
But what's that simmering?
Just under the surface.
It feels a little off.
It's probably nothing.
....Oh....
What's happening?
Is this an earthquake?
Breathe. It'll be OK.
This house is sturdy.
This house is strong.
It's weathered storms before.
But what is this house really built on???
....

Sand....Quicksand.
Are you ready for this?
It won't be easy.
My stakes are high and I require much.
Most people cower and run away in fear.
I demand your all and your every.
This is your last chance to put your head in the sand and hide.
....

No, I won't hide this time.
I am ready.
Let's go.
....

So how's that house?
Are you going to knock it down?
Think you'll rebuild?
Ha! Find solid ground.

You love your denial.
How's that been working?
You've allowed for years of 'good enough'.
Your denial is strong and you don't want to look.
Just open your eyes and I will help you to see.
I will lead you home and your truth will set you free.
....

I'm so confused, this can't be real.
How could this have happened?
Was it me?
Maybe I'll live in limbo, just until the shaking stops.
No! It's just too much.
This shaking won't end.
I feel queasy, limbo sucks.
Wait, there's some joy!?!
And a true connection! Yes!!!
Nope, never mind.
It was just a mask.
Now this feels empty, there's nothing here.
I'm all alone.
I did it wrong.
I must be lost.
I feel so used.
That truth, it hurts.
This is just torture.
It's not fair and I've had enough.
Though, I can't just give up?
But I want out...
Goddess, release me.
....

No, you can't leave.
We're not done.
You have work to do... you know what it is.
You see that shadow?

Yeah, that one there.
It ain't pretty.
Yes, it's yours.
It must be honored, it must be seen.
You must dissect it.
Yes, this gets messy.
But don't give up, we have time.
You'll get out alive… but first, this must die.

....

Huh? Wait what?!
You're joking right?!
I didn't sign up for this!
This can't die!
Look at this life, this beautiful life.
It's meant to be.
I love it here!
Well, most of the time.
I mean, it's comfortable.
I'm usually safe.
It's what I want, right???
Well, it's all I know.
What else is there?
Yikes! That sounds scary!
But could there be more?
Is there more?
Goddess, show me.

....

I am Goddess, the Queen of the Dark.
You set an intention to live in truth.
Don't mess with words because I'll see you keep them.
This is my journey.
I carved you this path and it's an honor you won't forget.
I am always here in your shadow,
in your truth,

in your fear,
in your pain,
in the void,
in the dark night of your soul.

I am Inanna.
I am Kali.
I am Pele.
I am Medusa.
I am Erishkigal.
I am Hecate.
I am Persephone.
I am you and you are me.
We are one and eternity.

Inanna of the Apple Tree, A Woman's Midrash[41] to the Goddess

Hayley Arrington

A prayer:
O glorious Inanna
You who are older than the word
Lady of the apple tree
Queen,
Bless this woman!

A story:
In your holy garden
You tended your tree,
But,
A serpent who could not be charmed
Settled in your roots,
The anzu-bird nested in your branches,
And the red maid Lilith shaped her home in your trunk.

This could not be abided.
You who tended to your apple tree so well,
You sought to reap its fruit
And wear blossoms in your hair.

---

41 Midrash, a form of biblical exegesis which literally means to investigate or study; a Jewish tradition of reinterpretation of original texts. Women's spiritual midrash has become an increasingly popular feminist form of reclaiming sacred texts from all different religious and mythological origins. In my midrash for Inanna, I reinterpret "The *Huluppu*-tree" poem to show Inanna overcoming her obstacles on her own and embracing her shadow self. I interpret the Huluppu-tree as an apple tree as a further way of embracing that symbol so closely allied with women's sin, for my own and other women's reintegration of our fears, and knowing that we can be all we need to be for ourselves.

Your queenly bed was to be made from its wood.
A bed to exalt your form;
Apple-scented sheets to caress your thighs,
To enwrap yourself within.
You, who never felt helpless,
Called for help from all quarters.

Your Goddess' throne was to be shaped
From its trunk
From the holy apple tree
From your holy garden.

Inanna, your cries went unanswered!
Your sovereignty was held hostage.
Held hostage by those creatures
In your branches
In your trunk
In your roots.

Lilith called your name
The anzu-bird sang to her chicks
The serpent slithered

The red maid beckoned.
She dried your tears.
"I am your fears,"
She whispered.
"I know," you replied.
Lilith crowned you with blossoms.
The birds sang your coronation song.
The serpent twined itself around your arm,
A fitting scepter.

You slept beneath your apple tree:
A natural bed.
You sat within its branches:
A natural throne.

You, who feared the unknown,
Who sought the end,
And feared the means;
You confronted,
You won,
You crowned yourself!

A prayer:
Inanna!
As you sought your Queenhood
And tended to your tree
I, too, seek to reap my own gifts
You overcame and wore your crown.
Lend your gifts of the apple to me
As I seek the wisdom of your star
Within your fruit
In the Morning and
In the Evening.
Ancient Goddess
You who are older than the word
Lady of the apple tree
Queen,
Bless this woman!

Abundant Inanna
Nuit Moore

'Abundant Inanna' from an in-progress oracle deck by Nuit Moore.

Sacrifice to Sovereignty:
A Healer's Real-Life Inanna Story

Melanie Miner

THINKING I WAS QUEEN

All my life I have been a healer. As far back as I can remember I was sensitive to energy, emotions, people, places and even animals. I knew that I could feel things many around me couldn't, and it affected me deeply. As I grew up, this sensitivity forged a deep desire to alleviate the pain and suffering I felt all around me and it led into an insatiable love affair with health and the healing arts.

I guess you could say that my "career" as a healer started after the birth of my son in my early twenties. Through this initiation, I was drawn into the world of midwifery and studied the birth arts to become a Doula. I loved being of service in this way and attended many home and hospital births. This eventually led into learning and teaching about all areas of women's health and wellness, from fertility and sexuality to menstruation and menopause. I also studied traditional whole foods, healing arts like herbal medicine, flower essence and essential oils; reclaimed women's spiritual mysteries; began holding women's circles and offering year-long initiate trainings... and eventually became the Ordained High Priestess that I am today.

I was heeding this calling on my heart to be of healing service.

For fifteen years I devoted myself to women's healing and empowerment and as a result held a prominent position in my community. I was known in 4 counties for what I offered. I even remember a time walking into my local health food store and having a woman say to me (rather loudly) after finding out who I was... "You are THE Melanie Miner???" While a bit embarrassing, that moment solidified for me that I had indeed built a solid reputation as a healer and wise woman.

I felt like I was living a dream.

I was on purpose, doing what I was created to do. As any healer will tell you, there is no better feeling... than that of living your purpose and contributing in our own unique way to healing on the planet. It's what we are born to do.

On the outside it looked like I had it all together. Women were coming from all over the state to attend my healing circles... my trainings, workshops and classes were always full... and, I never had to advertise.

But there was something else happening beyond what the eye could see. While it was clear that I was a gifted healer, sensitive to the needs of the women in my community, and well educated in feminine wisdom and wellness... underneath it all something was simmering... and it was about to boil over and change my entire life.

THE FALL

I remember it like it was yesterday. It was a warm Circle night in August 2011. We had just completed our Circle ceremony and women were packing up their belongings and saying their goodbyes. There was a select group of ladies, around eight or so, that had chosen to stay overnight in my Circle Bed and Breakfast. It happened that that a daughter of one of the circle attendees wanted to stay that night as well. She had a heart's desire to become a chef someday and wanted to help in the kitchen the next morning. I was ecstatic to receive the help and loved the idea of passing along kitchen wisdom to the next generation.

Unfortunately (or fortunately, as will become clear later in this story) the women choosing to stay didn't feel the same. As the news of this young girl's participation began to filter through the group, I could feel the stirrings of discontent. To make a long story short, these women ended up not staying, and caused quite a stir amongst all the ladies who witnessed their departure.

What ensued after that night I couldn't have possibly imagined and certainly wasn't prepared for. Allegations were made. Alliances shifted. Some women left our Circle and my business as a result. Personally, I was heartbroken and in a state of complete disbelief. I felt blindsided. I hadn't seen this coming, or hadn't I? I spend days questioning myself and going over it all again and again in my mind. What had I done that was so wrong? Should I have asked the young girl to leave? Should I have given them a full refund?

The hardest part was that these women were my community. Many lavished praise on me and my offerings, so why the sudden turn around? Didn't they understand this was my reputation and livelihood? Didn't they care?

I canceled my next month's Circle. I needed time. Time to reflect... time to feel... and time to heal. I knew something significant was happening and I didn't want to miss it or be distracted from the process of it.

I spent that month taking a deeper look into this experience and the feelings it triggered in me. For a woman who thought she had built such a rock-solid healing business in her community... I certainly wasn't feeling rock-solid, especially if something like this could trigger such a devastating downfall. There were obviously serious cracks in my foundation.

I had to get honest with myself and acknowledge that, while this situation was the most significant I had faced in my business as a healer... it certainly wasn't the first. There were signs. Little things here and there.

1. Students arriving late or ill prepared (or even under the influence)—that I let slide.
2. Clients that I embraced as "friends" only to realize later the imbalance of our relationship – that I let slide.
3. Times of saying yes when I should have said no—that I let slide.
4. Giving, and giving, and then giving some more—that I let slide.
5. Bartering, discounting and even giving away my services for free—that I let slide.

I'm embarrassed to say that the list of things "I let slide" was long... and taking this kind of inventory had been long overdue. Something was becoming very clear through this process—I wasn't the victim I thought I had been. While this group of women certainly had done some damage to my business, my reputation and my confidence... what was more disturbing was the hard to face fact that there was really only one person who had continually disrespected the gifts, the time, the love and the energy I placed into my work—and that person was me.

DESCENDING INTO THE UNDERWORLD

Time and time again I had allowed students to take advantage of me. Time and time again I had disregarded my own wellbeing to make others happy or more comfortable. I was the one who was tolerating bad behavior, charging well below my worth and working myself to the point of exhaustion.

The harsh truth was that:
1. I felt under-appreciated, undervalued and taken advantage of.
2. I was burnt out, exhausted and becoming resentful.

3. I was unwell and suffering with an undiagnosed thyroid condition.
4. I under-priced, discounted, bartered and even gave away my gifts.
5. I worked really, really hard for what felt like very little return.
6. I had a complete lack of professional boundaries.

I had to acknowledge that my foundation was faulty.

I had to dig deeper into the "why" of it all. Why did I allow all that I did? What was operating beneath the surface that somehow made all of this ok? One thing was for certain, I couldn't continue. Once a veil like this is removed and you see the truth of the illusions you are living, there's no going back.

Let's be honest... how you do one thing, is how you do EVERYTHING, and this faulty foundation wasn't only affecting my business... it was affecting my life... and it was time for a profound change.

I closed my business and left everything behind. I even moved out of State. I abandoned it all... an entire life that had taken me fifteen years to build. I no longer had an identity. I had no community. I had no reputation. I had no business. I had nothing.

BEING STRIPPED OF ALL THAT I KNEW

I plunged into the dark world of depression.

I felt like a failure. Who was I to think I could help women? For months I was aimless. It was a challenge to even get out of bed. These times were messy. Much like the caterpillar who disintegrates within the cocoon, when all that you know is dying, the process isn't pretty. There had been a death, and I was in mourning.

Yet, it was during this process, with nothing outside of myself to distract me, that I was able to see the "whole" of my Self for the very first time.

Not just my light—my healing gifts, my knowledge and passion for women's wisdom and wellness, my skills as a teacher and priestess—those were easy to see. It was my darkness that was coming up for review—my co-dependency, my lack of boundaries, my poverty consciousness, my willingness to suffer and sacrifice myself... all of it.

For the first time I saw ALL of me.

Here, in my darkest of days, I was being given the gift of coming face-to-face with the depth of my Self. The parts I was ashamed of. The parts that I had denied. My Shadow. The part of me that had really been running the show in my life and healing business.

> "She was all that I am not. All that I have hidden. All that I have buried. She is what I have denied.
> Ereshkigal, my sister. Ereshkigal, my shadow. Ereshkigal, myself." -Amy Sophia Marashinsky

FACING MY SHADOW

I had a choice. I could reject this revelation. Turn my back on the darkest, (and what I had deemed the most shameful) parts of myself. Or, I could embrace it. Me. All of me.

Turns out, this would require some time travel.

It required appreciating how most of us as healers aren't raised in environments where our sensitivity is recognized, honored and protected. Often the opposite is true. We suffer varying degrees of neglect, rejection, abandonment, abuse and betrayal... and while on a higher soul level we choose this path which results in becoming a source of great wisdom, healing power and inspiration for others—we're also left wounded and bound to beliefs about ourselves, and the value of our gifts. Neglect becomes Self-neglect. Abandonment becomes Self-abandonment. Betrayal becomes Self-betrayal.

It required understanding that choosing to be born a woman growing up within a timeline that has denigrated and denied the Feminine, meant being conditioned by and bound to old-world beliefs that taught us how our value is found only in the giving, being and doing for everything and everyone around us and severs us from our ability to receive.

It required acknowledging that the healing profession overall comes with its own conditioning about service as sacrifice and how poverty is pious, often leaving healing women in a chronic experience of being undervalued and underpaid.

It required excavating past life memories of being a priestess, nun and/or healer and the many lifetimes of persecution, torture, burnings, and banishment we've experienced, the effects which reside deep within our DNA contributing to our comfort with invisibility in order to remain "safe" and "alive."

And while each of these portals and their corresponding life experiences bestow great soul blessings, they also create vows/contracts/cords to beliefs and ways of being that hold us in bondage to unhealthy ways of being.

Vows like:

Sacrifice ~ Suffering ~ Invisibility ~ Poverty
All dark programs that keep us bound to a distorted view of Self-less-ness – where women of powerful healing potential are turned into women without a strong sense of Self. Women who willingly turn the ministry of Service into one of Self-Sacrifice...

which ends up keeping women healers undervalued, underpaid and unwell.

All of the old-world beliefs I had held, had to be replaced with New Paradigm Principles and Practices that placed the restoration of me at the center of my world...

It was time for this sensitive and sacred woman to become a devotee to Sovereignty.

BEING CREATED ANEW

> Sovereignty: supreme self-power; freedom over all external control especially our pre-set, sub-conscious conditioning; personal authority; self-government; self-rule

What was to follow was a six-year initiatory journey into what it really meant to be the Queen of my life, which meant uncovering the Queen Mysteries and Her Pillars of Sovereignty—each guiding me in cultivating New Paradigm Practices that supported me in becoming a woman who is Centered in Self.

I trained with Queenly women. I took their courses. I read their books. I participated in their programs. Every aspect of who I thought I was and who I represented myself to be was transformed. This wasn't a process of becoming someone else. It was about letting go of all of who I wasn't and giving my Self permission to fully embody the truth of who I had always been.

This process changed my entire life.

It restored my relationship with my feminine essence and reoriented my experience of my masculine energy... enabling me to trust my intuition, become vulnerable enough to receive and learn the art of reciprocity within my relationships.

It put me back at the center of my life and I became a devotee to sacred self-care, healing my thyroid condition, getting into the BEST shape of my life and becoming a fully embodied woman.

It cleared my poverty consciousness, realigned me to truth of who I AM and how abundance is my divine birth rite.

I got clear on my value, my unique gifts and the importance of my work in the world and the role I was to play.

It resurrected my experience of personal power... gone are the days of sacrificing my own needs and suffering for the sake of keeping harmony and I can't tell you how amazing it feels to say yes only when I feel it and no whenever I mean it.

THE ASCENT

It's safe to say that my life and business doesn't look the same.

And while the experience of being in the Underworld, (stripped bare of everything I thought I was and given the opportunity to look my Shadow Self deep in the eye) wasn't enjoyable and was in fact quite lonely and painful... it offered the most profound gift if I was willing to completely surrender to the process.

Because of my decent there has been an integration of opposites within me and as a result, not only has my life and business transformed, but I feel... for the first time in my life... whole.

As a result, I've made it my mission to support other women healers, empaths and light workers through the same awakening. Helping them come face to face with their "healer shadow," supporting them in breaking free from vows/contracts and elevating them out of light worker sacrifice and into light leader sovereignty.

The dark night of the soul is a profound gift... if you have the courage to die to who you thought you were... and surrender to being reborn into who you were created to truly be.

Of Ocean and Stars, Wildness and Sun
Iriome R. Martín Alonso

Of Goddess' Nature: Balance
Iriome R. Martín Alonso

When people ask who Goddess is, they normally bear in mind the gender-swapped version of a former deity they used to worship. Some may describe Her as all loving, all generous and 'benevolent,' a definition borrowed from their previous faith that has been carved into their very souls. Due to my experience with Her, I mostly disagree.

It is not that She is evil, either. Goddess is the silver edge between Light and Darkness; the perfect harmony of the night that comes after the day or the winter after summertime. She is not divided into two, but the cosmology that has reigned for so long has made us think that everything is dichotomic instead of a whole; that we must choose a side, but She is the balance among 'opposites' that celebrates and shifts from one to the other without denying or suppressing any.

I was loved once by a person who used to tell me that I was a creature of Light surrounded by evil Shadows, and that I should cast my glow so bright that all of them would disappear at once. He used to say I was made of moonlight that leaked through the treetops in a dark forest. They were severe moments of grief, and I felt like I was not myself at all, so his statement carried the purest of intentions but it did not help my issues: The concept that Darkness was dirty—something I had to get rid off, poisoned me. It was true, I carried it inside my soul like tendrils drowning my heart. I tried to fight so hard against it that I focused on spiritual practices that spoke of how we are Light beings imprisoned on flesh cages; I was obsessed with a vague past life memory whose golden-light-beauty haunted me until practically taking me into madness. And then, She came again from the forgotten realms of my shattered faithless core. So balanced, so Dark and so Brilliant at the same time: the Dark Goddess.

You see, we have been taught that Light is good and Darkness is evil, when in truth they both hold the capacities to each moral compass. We even have learned that they are opposed enemies instead of complementary halves. Light can be so bright that it might blind us so irrevocably that we do not know which road we are going through; we do things moved by the Light that can be truly horrible; we can be cruel and hurt others and ourselves, considering wrongly that we are doing the right thing. In Darkness, we can also come to reach the deepest, truest parts of ourselves; we can draw strength from what we consider our flaws and turn them into our strongest features; we can undertake life-changing decisions moved by the desperation of a surrounding Darkness that would eventually lead us to become who we really are.

The point is not about bringing our shadows to the Light to be aware of them, or vice versa, it is about traveling through that gloom realm organically, against the false belief that being all the time in a never ending summerland is what we have to hope for, for denying and aspect of ourselves is like mutilating a part of our being.

Goddess has the ability to come from a to this sides as She wishes because She is in perfect balance, one way or another. It is not that She is a deeply wise crone who has mastered all the secrets of humanity and life, but She is life itself. Nature is all generous when it gives us what we need to survive, but it might as well be a cruel hurricane that tears our houses from their foundations. It is in its nature to be cruel and generous equally, and none of these qualities diminishes the others.

The Dark Goddess imbricates all the murky-shady features of our very soul. She is the dark winged raven; the lonely-empowered sovereign Queen; the weeping child who hides in the shady corners of Her room and the mysterious witch that everybody have met, but no one knows. She is the subtle misty spirit of Morgana le Fay, who is both a miraculous healer and a wild, untamed destroyer; She is the loneliness of Ereshkigal in the depths of the Underworld, hating Her sister Inanna and mourning Her death while giving Her birth again and interchanging powers; She is the warrior spirited, blood thirsty, Morrigan, who brings decay but also the life that comes from it; She is the choice of Persephone, eating the pomegranate seeds and thus becoming the Queen of Hell, bringing balance to the seasons and turning into a self-right Goddess; She is the freedom of Lilith the demonized, whose freewill set Her away from and idealized, unreal paradise to bring Her to this true, earthy realm; She is the torch on the crossroad held by Hekate to light up our paths when we are lost in the labyrinth and the freezing cold of the two-faced-Hela, both gorgeous and loathsome but always kind with the death.

Can we reach Goddess' level of balance? We should strive toward it, but as humans, imbalance is imperative so growth will come. It is funny how all of us believe we are the center of the world when in reality, we are one of the multiple cells that form the body that Goddess, that existence, is. If Goddess is the Universe, the Earth is but an organ that forms Her and every single ocean or piece of land is part of Her skin; every single species of living creatures are but the bacteria that inhabit Her and contribute to Her functioning. Through Herstory, we have been born and died like dead cells that eventually must be replaced. Far from discouraging us, this should make us feel proud of being part of such an inspiring miracle.

The Dark Goddess is a very much feared aspect, because when we hold Her hand, it means that we have to take responsibility for everything that goes on in our lives, for everything we do, feel and how we respond to it. It is a painful and titanic task to be able to see yourself in Her obsidian mirror and acknowledge the hidden features that you already were aware of but have been denying so strongly for so long. You might hate the look that you receive back from your own reflection, but She gives you a safe space in which to experience each emotion to its fullest, without judgment, for She knows that emotions are in nature neutral and we are the ones that link tags to them: When you experience something truthfully and allow it to pass through and over you, then you have the choice of what stays and what is banished.

It is so pretentious that we see Goddess not only with a woman's shape, but also with a human-like consciousness. That is called anthropocentrism. Of course, as humans, we do need symbols to approach Goddess, and giving Her such human characteristics allows us to empathize with Her, making a cognitive shortcut to comprehend and relate to such a magnificent, abstract and unintelligible being, whose consciousness is far different than our own. She is part of us, of everything that exists, and so understanding the part of Her in us is not enough to get the whole of Her being that also lies in other creatures and in the vastly different ways that Nature expresses Herself. As long as we are aware of the symbols we are using to build a relationship with Her, all of them shall be welcomed. The issues of any belief system, or any other religion, come when the symbol replaces the concept it refers to.

Why is Goddess so necessary today? I believe Goddess gives us a spirituality that does not focus on another plane of reality that might or might not exist—but it advocates for an Earth-based connection, a way of life that is in harmony with any other living beings and the planet Herself. Being a child of the Goddess is about seeking harmony within yourself through the seasons, mirroring your own rhythms on the ones from the Earth and also the equilibrium among your own Light and Darkness so they become one. We do not know what is the truth of the afterlife, and we are unaware of the reality or the purpose of existence— but Goddess knows that the only life we are really masters of is this one we are currently experiencing. And so, Her goal is to help us to make the best out of it for ourselves and everything that surrounds us.

The Dark Goddess in particular, through Her many faces across mythologies, legends and cultures is that so needed catalytic figure that unleashed the ropes that have been tying us for so long. Unfortunately, She has been reduced to the role of villain in all the stories we have heard, and so our natural response to Her presence is that of fear, as it is natural to fear the unknown. The Dark Goddess path is one of surrender, of giving away control and all the mental constructs that have helped us to survive but most of the times kept us from fully living. Re-imagining Her and being aware of Her true nature without being blind to Her shades, is a way of knowing ourselves for real.

In a time in which the so-called progress has not only disconnected us from ourselves—but also from our very own home on this planet—Goddess is also a way of returning to an ecological consciousness so imperative now: To know how to deal with the way we have exploited Her resources and the other creatures and plants with whom we share this wonderful land. Loving Goddess not only as a Great Mother but also as a closer Lover, a dear Sister or a fragile Child we have to protect is a way of making sure we will not allow Her to suffer harm from us any longer. She is used to transmuting and has nurtured species far greater than we are; She has endured the severest conditions. She will surely adapt and evolve, but, will we follow Her? The most intelligent thing is to protect the way She takes care of us now.

Goddess is also crucial in a time in which feminism is spreading as a way of confronting inequality. She does not know of ethnic groups, gender or sexual orientations, but She perceives us all as equal. In a society that holds women, people with other genders and orientations and with different cultures and skin colours in such an inferior position that toxic dynamics of power, before led by religious beliefs, are now intrinsically embroidered into culture —Goddess is not only a source of healing but also an inspiration of empowerment. She has given me courage in my most desperate moments, and She gives purpose and a sense of hope to a modern existence that seems to be numb, in an eternal anesthesia that hollows us like empty Shells whose lack of inner content eventually makes us so weak that we crack.

Goddess celebrates vulnerability, She celebrates the falls and the rises, She adores difference, the endurance in moments of struggle and the compassion of a person that helps others due to empathy. She holds and loves everything that is repudiated by the outside world—because everything comes from Her. Considering something out of the norm or unnatural would be like believing that nature is imperfect just because some things are less common than others. There is as much beauty in the rarest and loneliest of flowers as there is in a field full of the same plant.

What is Goddess? How is Goddess? Who is Goddess? Why is She important? Is She Dark, Light or Balanced? No scholar or paper, no priestess or wise person will ever answer it properly enough for you, such is the blessing and the burden of a path that cheers self-discovery like this does. But I promise that even though it might seem slow, frustrating and unpractical, nothing compares with the joy of experiencing Her not only around all of you, but also growing inside your very soul.

Inanna Blue
Vicki Scotti

Serpentine like pathways, transforming and disguised
Take me as I travel this darkened road, uncivilized
Am I who I seem to be, faceless & unknown?
Unexplored, undefined, far away from home
Inanna Blue, magical are you! Place your veils around me,
wrapped in midnight's hue, Transformative awakenings, Inanna Blue!

Challenges to rise above the ashes of demise
Changes within stirring, haunting, stalking me with watchful eyes
Growth that comes from deep within, changing my worldview
Unadorned, invincible, making me brand-new
Inanna Blue, magical are you! Place your veils around me,
wrapped in midnight's hue, Transformative awakenings Inanna Blue!

Seeking out that which we fear, embracing what's unknown
Emerging from the foggy depths, tranquility is now my home
Peaceful understanding feeds my troubled soul
Leading me on this path in this recurring role.
Inanna Blue, magical are you! Place your veils around me,
wrapped in midnight's hue Transformative awakenings Inanna Blue!

©2004 Vicki Scotti

Dancer Astarte dancing to *Inanna Blue*.

You Are Inanna

DeAnna L'am

On the day of your first Moon Blood—you were re-born as Inanna: She who travels between the worlds...

On your first Moon—you begun to journey with Her, through Her, as Her. When your Blood started flowing—Inanna took your hand and became your Guide for the journey: down into the Underworld, and back again. Every Moon, every Month -- for years to come... On that day—you became a Cyclical Being, guided by the Moon: expanding and contracting, descending and ascending... Anew with each cycle.

Inanna calls you to embody Her monthly. She leads the way through the darkness, if you only follow:
As your womb prepares to shed its inner lining, like a snake shedding its skin, it's time to go inward. Inanna is preparing you for the journey down into the Underworld, into the realm where intuition rules, where fluidity is the meandering path. This is your MoonTime: time to leave linearity behind, to turn off the light of reason, to surrender to the unknown, and to trust. Inanna's torch is shining in the dark. Can you follow it's trail?

Veil by veil she strips you of the month that has just ended. It's time to let go of the cycle that's gone. Release its joys and its disappointments. Don't cling on to what could-have sprouted but didn't... Don't hold-on to the fruits you have harvested... Each interrupted seedling carries a teaching. Each juicy fruit holds nectar that feeds you. As you begin your descent into the underworld stop to savor each: the sting of the teaching and the sweetness of the fruit. Then, take time to release them all. To bury the withered leaves, the fading petals, and the remains of the fruit that nourished you. Take them off like jewelry. Approach the underworld lighter and lighter, as you shed one layer after another.

Enter the underworld naked, like Inanna. With no expectations, no pride, no plans. Only your true essence can pass through this gateway. Only your naked heart can meet Ereshkigal—your counterpart: She who is shaped by Change.

Ereshkigal invites you to mourn with her, in the darkness, for all the aborted projects, the interrupted blooms, the pain that was caused by the world—to you or to other living beings. This darkened Underworld cavern is where you can safely cry... moan... lament... This is where the Great Mother can hold you in her arms and gently rock you. Your pain belongs here. You can't take this pain back with you, into the coming cycle, or it will bog you down and keep you in the Underworld. Let yourself feel it to its fullness, in order for it to dissolve. Let yourself experience the pain, and the Great Mother will comfort you.

It will take as long as it takes: An hour. A day. Your entire bleeding period. Or an instant. Your womb is calling you to tend to her, as she sheds her inner lining, as she bleeds the blood of life, as she releases another cycle.

Once Ereshkigal's sorrow is consumed, your pain will subside. It will give way to hope. It will make room for the New to come in: new ideas, fresh initiatives, brand new projects. A new cycle is being born. It's time to begin your departure from the Underworld. Adorn yourself with new veils and new jewels, as you trace the steps that brought you here, ascending back into your daily life.

Clad yourself with hope, as Inanna leads the way to a fresh new beginning. Gather new seeds to plant in the coming month. Grow them in the new cycle, and foster them into flowers and fruits as the cycle unfolds.

The new cycle will bring unimaginable gifts. Some sweet, some not. But you will not be swept out of orbit by one, nor crushed to the ground by the other, for you know the cycles repeat every Moon. Each Moon will bring an opportunity to plant again, to harvest and to bury, with Inanna at your guide!

You are Inanna. You expand and contract with the moon. You descend into the underworld to mourn, to shed, and to release. You leave behind what doesn't serve you. You surrender to the Great Mother's love and comfort. You gather your courage and strength, and you ascend again. And again. Every month. For you are a woman. You are a cyclical being. You are a spiral dance!

The Sacred Marriage Text
Translated by Miriam Robbins Dexter Ph.D.

From "The Sacred Marriage Text" – Sumerian Fragment, recorded 2000-1500 BCE.[42]

> . . . I am the queen of Heaven ...my husband ... the wild ox, Dumuzi ...
> Inanna ... [sings] a song about her vulva ...
> "[my] vulva ... like a horn ... the ship of Heaven ... like the new crescent moon
> I, the young woman, who will plant it?
> My vulva ... I, the queen, who will place the bull?"
> "Lady, let the king plant it for [you]; let Dumuzi, the king, plant [it] for [you]."
>
> [Dumuzi is] "...the honey of my eye; he is the lettuce of my heart."

> . . . ga-ša-an-an-na me-[e] ... mu-ud-na-mu ... am-^{d}dumu-zi ...
> ^{d}inanna-ke$_4$ ... SAL-la-ni sir-ra ... SAL-la ... si-gim ...
> ma-an-na ... u$_4$-sar-gibil-gim ... ki-sikil-mèn a-ba-a ur$_x$-ru-a-bi SAL-la-mu ...
> ga-ša-an-mèn gu$_4$ a-ba-a bí-íb-gub-bé in-nin$_9$ lugal-e ḫa-ra-an-ur$_x$-ru
> ^{d}dumu-zi lugal-e ḫa-ra-ur$_x$-ru.
>
> igi-mà làl-bi-im... šà-mà ḫi-(is)^{sar}-bi-im

---

42 The Sumerian text is in Samuel Noah Kramer, "Cuneiform Studies and the History of Literature: The Sumerian Sacred Marriage Texts." *Proceedings of the American Philosophical Society* (*PAPS*) 107.6, pages 505 and 508.

Madonna
Melissa Stratton Pandina

Seeking Sovereignty in the Land of the Dead
Carolyn Lee Boyd

What if the Underworld is a temple that we can visit while living? What if the Great Below is where we must venture to gain the power to become fully human?

Thirty years ago, in a small theater in New York City's American Museum of Natural History, author and storyteller Diane Wolkstein performed the myth of Inanna. With inspired tones and gestures, she made those ancient verses of the great Goddess of Sumer come alive.

"From the Great Above, the Goddess opened her ear to the Great Below...Inanna abandoned heaven and Earth to descend to the Underworld."[43] Overwhelmed by the deep reverberation of those mighty words, in a space within me that I had not known existed, I fell in love with the Goddess at that moment. In the very marrow of my bones, I knew that this story of metamorphosis was also my own.

In the myth, Inanna travels to the Underworld to witness the funeral of her brother-in-law, the husband of her sister Ereshkigal, Goddess of the Underworld. At Ereshkigal's command, she is stripped at each of seven gates to the Underworld of all the clothes and jewels that are symbols of her station as Queen of Heaven and Earth. She is condemned by the judges of the Underworld, then murdered by her wrathful sister. After her rotting corpse is hung on a meat hook for three days, she is rescued when the God of Wisdom sends two tiny beings to find her and bring her back to life. Inanna then ascends to her own realms: healed, wise, and fearless.

---

[43] Diane Wolkstein and Samuel Noah Kramer, *Inanna: Queen of Heaven and Earth, Her Stories and Hymns from Sumer,* New York, Harper&Row, 1983, p. 52.

In my life, portals to the realm of the Goddess of Death have not been grand and gilded gates. Rather, they have been small openings that I fall into now and again, unawares, only to be ejected back into the world of the living just as unexpectedly. These descents have been sometimes dramatic—and often just a bit odd.

If I skip over three just-in-the-nick-of-time emergency surgeries, the falling of a gigantic, ancient tree just a few yards from where I was peeling onions in the kitchen, and several other relatively mundane experiences, here are a few of the most memorable escapes.

A Charmed Life? As a teenage au pair in London in the 1970s, I decided at the last minute not to get on a subway train: one that was bombed by the Irish Republican Army a short time later. In my twenties, I walked home from work in eerie, peaceful silence at just the precise moment that the literal eye of the storm—a violent hurricane — was passing over New York City. A few months later, a gigantic plate glass window shattered only a few inches away from me, blown in by a powerful gust of wind. The dagger-sharp shards that scattered throughout the tiny room in which I was working missed me entirely. Some years later, I walked away unscathed when an airplane on which I was a passenger barely avoided several lightning bolts that hit the runway just as it was about to land. The pilot—who miraculously wrenched the plane out of its flight path and almost straight up to avoid the storm—was stunned. "I can't believe we made it," he unknowingly commented into his open microphone after we landed. A few years later, I was in a parked car when another vehicle, spinning wildly on ice, came within inches of smashing into my car door.

These close calls started to happen in my teens, and I eventually came to believe that I was just a wee bit invincible. That impression brought with it a profound sense of freedom. Fate, I concluded, was repeatedly protecting me from the chaos that was seemingly all around, but miraculously passed over me. As a result, I no longer felt bound to the expectations and demands of life as a young woman in late 20th century mid-America.

If I actually died, I mused, then there would be no Carolyn to act, believe, speak, and live according to what was expected by society. So, since the world should have been bereft of my existence anyway, I was now liberated to be precisely—and only—who I chose to be.

Creating My Own Adventure. I became my own Goddess of Creation, taking the opportunity to create my life as I wanted it. Like an artist, I started with a vision of what I would like to look like in this version of my life and went from there. I imagined what my day would be like, and how I would make a living, and then set about fashioning that existence.

At age twenty-two, I left my secure, suburban midwest home to recreate myself as a punk poet in the East Village of New York City. I dressed in a black velvet opera cape, dyed my hair red, and engaged in street poetry performance art. A few years later, taking on a completely different persona, I married and moved to a history-soaked small town in New England. While there, I renovated a ramshackle Victorian house, went to grad school, got a professional job, and raised a family. Since then, I have remade myself in smaller ways many times: changing my hair and wardrobe to fit whatever part I am playing, taking up hand drumming in my fifties in preparation for maybe being a street musician as an encore career, switching between being an herb-growing hedge witch on the weekends and a suit-wearing manager on weekdays.

To my youthful self, sovereignty was the ability to make my life be exactly as I wished. In the decades since then, I have learned that this ability to create (and recreate) oneself is a privilege that is much harder won for many than it was for me, especially for women who patch together their existences in spite of violence, poverty, illness, or prejudice.

I once spoke to a woman who had lost her family, her village and her country through war, had grown up in a refugee camp and had eventually found her way to the U.S. where she now struggles day to day to feed and clothe her family. "I keep on and don't get angry, what good would that do?" she said. I now realize that my younger self only played at a shallow form of sovereignty, while many others survive by wresting their own sovereignty out of next to nothing every day.

Facing the Underworld, Not Just Playacting. Once Inanna shed her clothes and jewels and entered the Land of the Dead, she was judged and killed, truly facing death. As much as I had thought about my own death over the first half-century of my life, I was far from actually confronting it.

However, one bright winter day when I was 55, I found myself unexpectedly lying in my upstairs hallway, slipping in and out of consciousness due to loss of blood from a sudden hemorrhage. I was oddly calm, and remember wondering if the ambulance would arrive in time. I thought this was just another quick trip to the edge, but instead, during the emergency surgery that followed, it was revealed that I had cancer. Now I, too, had to face the possibility that I would be subject to Inanna's fate: this time, for real.

At first I clung to my fantasy of immortality, and I tried desperately to convince myself that I was different from everyone else in the cancer center waiting room. Was I not the creator of my own life, sovereign over my fate? But with every infusion bag draining into my body, every night spent awake from drug-induced bone pain, radiation burns, and every dinner out spent sick in the ladies room, my hubris gradually wore away. Like Inanna, listening to the charges against her, knowing that her conviction was a foregone conclusion, I finally accepted that I, too, would die one day.

I came to the bone-deep realization that my death might not be from cancer, and might not be imminent, but it truly was inevitable. I became overwhelmed by panic and was not living well—whether for weeks or decades.

I challenged myself to regain what sovereignty I had for the time that remained to me—however long that might be. What I found after I came to this conclusion surprised me. During my few weeks of treatment, whenever I entered the cancer center, I imagined that I was entering a true-to-life Land of the Dead, where everyone would be grim, resigned, and depressed—just like me. Yet, after I started coming to terms with my ordeal, I began to observe that most of the people around me did not behave as if they were anticipating that they would soon being denizens of the Underworld. Many had large families with them and would spend the long hours of chemotherapy infusion lunching on pizza and chatting. No one was crying. Most were talking and even laughing, reading magazines or scolding fidgety children. They were acting as if their lives were not on the edge of annihilation. What did they know that I did not?

Rescued by the Helpers. I was puzzled by the attitudes of the other patients in the cancer center, and sought answers in Inanna's story. What, I pondered, made it possible for her to rise up from the Underworld? Her rescuers were two small beings, tinier than fleas, who had been sent by the God of Wisdom to brave the terrors and dangers of the Underworld to bring Inanna home. They won her release by moaning empathetically with Ereshkigal in her absolute and unrelenting misery, moving that dire goddess to offer them whatever they wished in gratitude. They asked for Inanna's corpse, which they brought back to life. Inanna's ascent to a deeper, wiser divine existence was made possible by the same kind, simple caring that is repeated by humans and other living beings all over the world, billions of times a day.

In the days following my diagnosis, I was inundated with love from so many people. My husband came to any appointment I wished, my sister traveled 800 miles to weep with me, my work colleagues banded together to cover for me so I could take the time to recover, and friends and acquaintances sent cards, letters, and lots of advice. My own rescue into remission was made possible by the hundreds of medical researchers who dedicate their lives to finding cures—and by doctors, nurses, and other medical professionals who devised the right treatments and delivered them in a way that let me know I was more than just my disease.

My beaten-down, terrorized, and weary heart was eventually uplifted by the kindness and compassion that was shown in spite of—or even due to—my suffering. The trappings of my new life—the pain, exhaustion, and uncertainty—were real, but were not what defined me. My sovereignty transformed from my childlike ability to dress up in new lives like a doll, to the deeper, richer power of being part of a web of human connection. I could not determine what would happen to me, but I could choose to be part of a community that has sovereignty over what kind of a world we all live in. Perhaps those other patients had experienced a similar kind of epiphany.

What is True Sovereignty? I now understand that sovereignty does not mean always being regal. Yes, there is a form of sovereignty that means understanding our worth; speaking and acting with the authority; and demanding what is right for ourselves, others, and the Earth. However, an essential element of our human sovereignty is also finding the power in quietly nurturing each other in everyday ways. We also express sovereignty by treasuring each dawn, and knowing that we have it in our power to make the world better before we go to sleep again. In being grateful for our flesh-and-blood bodies (even as they become more fragile), we realize how necessary it is for us to be alive together and relate to one another.

Our sovereignty is more hard-earned than that of an immortal Goddess. We are human, and as such, mortal. It takes deep courage, caring, and wisdom to be sovereign as a mortal being, sovereign when with others, to realize, at the deepest possible level, that we will choose not what length, type, or form of life we will have, but only who we will be as people even in the face of vulnerability and the inevitable end to our current form of existence.

I'm now four years into remission, with the chance of recurrence remote and a new immunotherapy for my type of cancer now available. While I no longer contemplate death daily, I still hope to have more visits to the Underworld before my last journey there. But I believe I have come to a time when I no longer need to stumble into the portals because I can find ways to go through them voluntarily—in meditation, in making creative works, in assisting others as they transition to Ereshkigal's realm—not forever but for just a moment to gain a needed insight, clarity, or understanding. The Underworld is not, I have learned, the place where the last remnants of our true selves go when we are annihilated from the Earth, but is instead a place that is as close as our imaginations and our legacy of Goddess stories, found in the American Museum of Natural History, a hospital room, a street or office, or anywhere we may happen to be at this moment. It is a place that holds the keys to our special human and mortal sovereignty—if we will only journey there to seek it.

Originally published as "My Journey with Inanna" in SageWoman #93, "Sovereignty: Claiming Our Power." For more information or to purchase this issue see www.sagewoman.com or call 503-430-8817.

Inanna, Above & Below
Laura Tempest Zakroff

Featured in n SageWoman #93, "Sovereignty: Claiming Our Power."

Inanna in the Armenian Dance of the Reed

Laura Shannon

Introduction: Descent

Even as a young girl, I admired the older girls and women in my life—my sister, my mother, my grandmothers and aunts—and instinctively felt there was something special about being a woman, which I was proud to be part of and eager to grow into. At the same time I was keenly aware that my blossoming femininity made me a target, and my childhood was punctuated by frightening encounters in which I found myself in danger because I was female.

In our time, we are able to speak openly about our experiences of sexual threat, assault, or abuse, and to see how tragically frequent they are for so many young women and girls in our society. In the United States of the 1970s, however, I felt completely and utterly alone. These unwanted encounters left me with a terrible sense of shame, which I internalised and translated into deep feelings of powerlessness, inadequacy and worthlessness. My early years as a young woman were marked by descent: depression, despair, chronic health problems, and an overall sense of being lost, not fitting in. There was nobody to show me healthy self-love and self-care, nobody to teach me how to safely grow up as a woman in a woman-hating world.

The intensity of my descent brought me into contact with various sources of support. Sylvia Brinton Perera's book, *Descent to the Goddess*, gave me great inspiration and comfort early on.[44] I was astonished to see my lonely journey of depression and exile reflected in a myth of female initiatory descent and return dating back more than 4,000 years. The figure enacting this archetypal

---

44 Perera 1981.

cycle, the Goddess Inanna, was the central female deity of her era[45], but this was the first I had heard of her.

The hymns to Inanna, written ca. 2300 BCE by the priestess-poet Enheduanna and beautifully translated by Betty De Shong Meador, revealed that Inanna's gifts include not only the acceptance, but the celebration of female sexuality as a precious treasure, worthy of protection.[46] Inanna embodied, in Meador's words, 'what so many women long for, a spirituality grounded in the reflection of a divine woman, offering a full sense of foundation and legitimacy as females.'[47] I hoped it was not too late for me to learn this too.

My quest to reconsecrate my wounded femininity led me to the healing power of dance. I trained in both dance movement therapy and Sacred Dance, and began to research traditional women's circle dances of the Balkans. That was more than thirty years ago. Since then, my personal ascent has been mediated through movement, both solo and shared, which has accompanied an epic journey of inner work throughout my entire adult life.

Armenian Traditional Dance

Among traditional women's dance forms, I was particularly moved by Armenian dances. Their poignant melodies, connection to nature, and timeless gestures expressing love, longing and homecoming, helped me rediscover and express something previously silent, deep in my soul.

---

45 Meador 2009: 133.
46 I was amazed to learn in Meador's book that Enheduanna was the earliest known poet to be recorded by name, though I had not learned about her in my studies of history and literature.
47 Meador 2000: 9.

In their healing capacity and the effect they have on our body, mind and spirit, I found a link between Armenian lyrical dance movements and the body-based spiritual practices of yoga, T'ai Chi and Qi Gong. All of these movement arts generate a gentle yet powerful energy, the beneficial life force variously known as *prana, shakti, väki, mana, chi* or *qi*.[48] In dance, we experience this as a perceptible warmth, not from vigorous athletic exertion, but rather from movements which gently stimulate the energy meridians in the body.[49]

Armenian lyrical dance draws on a vocabulary of ancient movements inspired by trees, animals, birds and elements of nature. The inherent spirituality of nature is also emphasised in Armenian Christianity: The Armenian cross, the *khachkar*, depicts a Tree of Life rather than a crucifix, a symbol of living wisdom rather than an instrument of suffering. Since antiquity, the Tree of Life has been connected with the Goddess, who was honoured in Armenia as in the rest of the ancient world. Names of the ancient Armenian Goddess included Saris, Anat, Anahit, Nar, and Nune or Nane, whose name reveals her connection to Sumerian Inanna, with whom she shares key attributes.

When Armenian women dance to lyrical folk music, each woman typically dances alone, freely improvising her solo expression on the theme of the dance, drawing on a common language of gestures dating back to pre-Christian times. In recent generations, lyrical dances have come to be choreographed in a circular form, so that many women can dance these dances together.

In London, where I was living in the late 1980s, I was fortunate to find a wonderful teacher, Shakeh Major Tchilingirian, who has become a dear friend and colleague. Shakeh is an acclaimed solo performer known for her interpretation of the Armenian folk lyrical dance style, and has brought many lyrical circle dance

---

48 Shannon 2017b: 71.
49 Shannon 2018.

choreographies into the world, drawing on beloved elements of Nature which carry a symbolic meaning for Armenian women, including sacred trees such as pomegranate, apricot, and cherry, or birds and animals including the swan, crane, white dove, and deer. Each lyrical dance is based on the ancient improvised language of traditional movements invoking a specific animal, bird, or tree, in order to bring their unique qualities into the human realm. Then as now, the woman dancing is also a woman praying, bringing a blessing from the realms of nature into the human world. The beautiful, graceful, harmonious movements in unison help dancers align with these benevolent powers of nature and practice new and healthier ways of thinking, moving, and seeing.

One of Shakeh's most poignant and powerful lyrical dance arrangements is inspired by the reed. It is set to a traditional love song, Dou im Yeghek ('You, My Reed'), in which the reed is a metaphor for the beloved.[50] The reed is also an ancient symbol of survival which shows us how to bend and not break. Never growing singly, it represents community strength and solidarity. Despite its yielding appearance, it is deeply rooted and cannot be torn up with bare hands. Growing at the edge of rivers and lakes, reeds stabilise the land, provide shelter and shade, nurture wildlife and enrich the environment. Reeds also cleanse the water they grow in.

Inanna and the Reed

The reed was integral to the development of early Mesopotamian civilization, where Armenian culture also originated. In the vast marshlands between the Tigris and Euphrates rivers, reeds provided food, shelter, boats, houses, baskets, mats, paper, cloth,

---

50 The music is arranged by Khatchatur Avetissian, one of Armenia's most influential composers and arrangers of traditional music. He used traditional Armenian instruments and melodies to support the expression of the dancers' soul and the beauty of nature.

torches, and other essential items.[51] Although Sumerian mythology had a designated goddess of reeds—Ningal, 'the great lady,' whose husband was the moon god Nanna-Sin—the reed was also intricately associated with the Goddess Inanna.[52] Before the development of cuneiform script, the Sumerian hieroglyph of a reed knot was Inanna's original sign.

This hieroglyph, depicting a bundle of reeds curved into a circle, appears on numerous religious objects from prehistoric Mesopotamia, as early as 4000-3350 BCE.[53] Also known as Inanna's Knot, it appears to be linked with similar symbols—including the Egyptian *ankh* and *tyet*, the Minoan sacral knot and labyris, as well as the astrological sign for Venus, the planet associated with Inanna. In some early pictographs, the reed bundle looks like a priestess, with long hair and outstretched hands.[54]

The reed post with the knot at the top may derive from the symbol of the tree of life or world tree, the celestial pole connecting heaven, earth, and the underworld.[55] A pair of them served as gateposts for the temple or the storehouse—also made of reeds—where grain, young animals, and valuables could be safely stored. The two top loops held a crossbar from which a mat was hung to form a door. In this way, Inanna's sacred knot or reed circle 'signified Inanna's position as guardian of the abundant harvest kept in the communal storehouse. As a doorpost, Inanna guards the passageway between two worlds, the outside ordinary world and the inside sacred womb-shaped sanctuary that shelters the abundant harvest.'[56] The sacred area of the storehouse or

---

51 Maxwell 1933.
52 Perera 1981: 66.
53 Meador 2000: 190.
54 Falkenstein 1936, cited in Meador 2000: 12.
55 Meador 2000: 16.
56 Meador 2000: 14.

gipar was probably also a birthing hut,[57] and 'was essentially a place for women.'[58]

As Meador points out, the marshland was a 'liminal space separating the river waters and dry land. The doorway to the storehouse marked the transitional space between secular outside and hallowed inside' so that Inanna's emblem 'heralded the entrance into that special state of mind called the sacred'.[59] Perera affirms that Inanna 'symbolises consciousness of transition and borders, places of intersection and crossing over that imply creativity and change.'[60]

Traditional Armenian dances also usher us into a special state of mind. The act of mirroring movements found in nature—plant, animal, wind, or water—is an archaic means of bringing their blessings into the human world. It is easy to see the link here to early shamanistic practices of Central Asia; Sumerian ritual practices, too, show evidence of links to ancient shamanism.[61] Present-day circles of women all over the world are finding that women's ritual dances—Armenian, Balkan, or Greek – offer 'an embodied spiritual practice which can nurture and guide their inner process,' in which they 'may receive personal insight and understanding, and connect to sources of healing energy and ancient wisdom.'[62]

Shakeh Tchilingirian's arrangement of the Armenian Dance of the Reed, Dou Im Yeghek, has been just such an ever-deepening journey for me. Long-term practice of this dance has brought me a wealth of insights and a deeper understanding of the Goddess Inanna, which I would like to share here. My interpretation does not necessarily reflect the choreographer's original intention; nor

---

57 Meador 2000: 63.
58 Meador 2000: 65.
59 Meador 2000: 15.
60 Perera 1981: 16.
61 van Dijk 1969, cited in Meador 2000: 15.
62 Shannon 2017a: 58.

does it need to, as traditional dance movements, like other nonverbal art forms, can accommodate diverse interpretations. Every dancer's experience 'has its own unique meaning: We dance the same dances, but travel to different places within as we do so'.[63] In this way, traditional dance movements are like the polyvalent patterns and symbols found in early Neolithic artefacts, able to transmit multiple meanings simultaneously on many levels.[64]

I will accompany my descriptions of the dance movements with excerpts from Betty Meador's translations of hymns to Inanna which relate to my experience.

The Dance of the Reed

We begin in an alert stance, with palms of the hands and soles of the feet awake to receiving earth energies from below. This mirrors the conscious receptivity of Inanna, her 'active willingness to receive.'[65] We open our arms out to the sides and lift them up like wings, until the right arm stretches up, like the upright reed, while the left curves over our head, with a sharp bend at the elbow, like the broken reed. The broken reed serves a valuable purpose, giving support to the upright reeds and shelter to birds and animals who make their home in the reedbed. Brokenness has a place in the cosmic order of things: It evokes compassion and can bring wisdom, just as Inanna was broken by her journey to the underworld, yet found in her experience a source of wisdom and power. The upright reed signifies the part of us that survives it all unscathed: 'Inanna's tall reed standards stand like insurgent flags amid the bastion of traditional beliefs that restrict women.'[66] Together, upright and broken reed offer an affirmation of wholeness. The invitation is to accept ourselves and each other as

---

63 Shannon 2016a: 6.
64 Gimbutas 1989, Christ 2017, cited in Shannon 2017b: 65.
65 Perera 1981:13.
66 Meador 2000: 10.

we are, including the parts that have journeyed to the underworld.

For each of us has indeed been through an underworld journey. Illness, depression, betrayal, the loss of loved ones, and the daily contempt thrown at women and girls in a society where misogyny has been normalised: These and many other challenges may send us to the underworld. None of us can avoid these periodic descents, which are a key part of woman's experience, but we can hope, like Inanna, to survive and return transformed.

The Dance of the Reed progresses with long slow steps and deep knee bends which hint at the descent to come. With tiny knee bends like ripples at the water's edge, we turn to greet the four directions, inviting the order and harmony of the cosmos – Inanna's upper realm, the heavens or Upper Waters – to come into the human world, the Lower Waters, Inanna's earthly realm. We stretch out both arms as we offer this blessing to the landscape and the Goddess.

> *Inanna*
> *godly maiden ripened on earth*
> *YOU ARRIVE*
> *your spread-out arms*
> *wide as the Sun King*[67]

In the second part, we move forward quickly in a straight, unhesitating, direct path forward.

> *to smooth the traveler's road*
> *to clear a path for the weak*
> *are yours Inanna*
> *to straighten the footpath*

---

67 Meador 2000: 92.

> *to make firm the cleft place*
> *are yours Inanna*[68]

Our flowing movement sustains a posture with uplifted breast, reminiscent of waterbirds such as swans, geese, and cranes, which are also associated with Aphrodite, the Greek iteration of Inanna. Both goddesses were associated with erotic cosmic power, the great motivating force for the continuation of life, and both were associated with the dawn and evening star—the planet Venus, known in Greek as *Afrodíti*.

The movements in this part of the dance express grace, strength, and the power of flight. We are reminded of the winged woman, archetypal figure of the priestess and the Goddess. Inanna herself was often depicted with wings and associated with birds as well as serpents, all symbols of the ancient Goddess of Life, Death and Regeneration. In Greek mythology, the original female figure with wings is the Goddess Ananke (Ἀνάγκη), 'Necessity,' the 'primeval goddess who emerged at the beginning of time, creating herself as a snake-like being of pure energy... the embodiment of a transpersonal fate that balanced the actions of gods and men... [and] kept everything within set limits.'[69] Inanna too shares these attributes, as a goddess of 'Time, Fate, Natural Order and Harmony.'[70]

After the movement expressing the bird's flight, a gesture of gathering in front of the heart signifies the bird's nest.

> *to build a bird's nest*
> *safe in a sound branch*
> *make indestructible*
> *are yours Inanna*

---

68 Meador 2000: 126-7.
69 Wosien 2017: 41-44.
70 Silvermoon 2012.

...

*to gather the scattered
restore the living place
are yours Inanna*[71]

With this protective gesture, we make a full turn—symbolic of transformation—in seven steps which rise and fall, up and down, as if crossing the threshold between the upper and lower worlds. The seven steps recall the seven gates through which Inanna passes on her descent to the underworld. There she must surrender her ceremonial adornments, and finally her life itself. Perera points out that Inanna's 'seven garments of queenship lie on her body at the levels of the kundalini chakras,'[72] indicating an initiatory energetic awakening. The seven gates through which Inanna must pass twice also reflect the seven lunar conjunctions the planet Venus makes as it progresses through its phases as Morning and Evening Star. Through this process of transformation, something survives when all else is sacrificed: This is the wisdom found in the Underworld. We repeat the full turn in seven steps in the opposite direction, illustrating Inanna's return.

We renew contact with the upper world and its rhythms of sun and moon, night and day, in an interlude reflecting the timeless landscapes of Mesopotamia. Our hands form a circle to show the full moon reflected in the abundant water, then rising high in the sky. After our underworld journey, we are renewed by 'the waters that restore the wasteland, symbolic of the never-ending flow of life's energies.'[73]

Our hands reach up in an ancient Zoroastrian gesture of sun worship, which is one of the oldest Armenian dance movements known. Here the dancer is the priestess carrying a message

---

71 Meador 2009: 130.
72 Perera 1981: 61.
73 Perera 1981: 68.

between earth and sky: a message of love and the life force, the universal charge of desire which through sun and rain and *eros* makes all things grow. In Meador's words, this is how Inanna 'transports the fundamental force of desire from heaven to earth. The poet places sensuality and desire at the heart of the cosmos. The life force itself is energized by desire.'[74]

Ascent

In the final movement of the dance, the group comes together in a tightly woven circle, like a woven basket of reeds. Our knees are bent, our feet firmly planted on the ground: we form an enclosed courtyard, a protected city, a 'firm-anchored house'.[75] Each dancer is a tall and graceful reed post, a circle of pillars creating a sacred space.

> *...godly pillars*
> *beautiful as queens*[76]

Each dancer extends her left arm behind her neighbour and places her hand gently in the centre of the back, at the level of the solar plexus chakra, seat of will and power in the energy body. The right arm extends up and out, with the hand circling first over her own crown chakra, then above the crown of the woman to her right.

> *over the maiden's head*
> *she makes a sign of prayer*[77]

Blessings flow through our hands and arms, woven together in this beautiful circle. We both receive and give the gifts of protection and healing. As Bessel van der Kolk affirms, 'our capacity to destroy one another is matched by our capacity to heal

---

74 Meador 2009: 120.
75 Meador 2009: 32.
76 Meador 2000: 95.
77 Meador 2000: 123.

one another';[78] this act of mutual healing is the key to recovery from trauma.[79] We have all been to the underworld, and are stronger because of it. Our very brokenness brings us closer as a community, in shared support and strength.

We look around, sharing a gaze that is full of tenderness and love, honouring our experience and all of our parts, both broken and whole. Sumerian poetry calls this gaze the "eyes of life": 'seeing that is full of love and gives vitality.'[80] We witness the miracle of our survival, and honour each other's willingness to 'dare the descent,' as 'many modern women are called upon by their dreams and feelings to do.'[81]

Conclusion: Safe Space

Armenian dances help us reconnect with the joy of community, the powers of nature, the harmony of the cosmos, and our own part in it all. 'They strengthen our capacity for resilience, forgiveness, and healing, and help us connect to one another and to ourselves. They open our hearts.'[82]

> *You of the bountiful heart*
> *You of the radiant heart*
> *I will sing of your cosmic powers*[83]

Inanna's epithet, 'Lady of Largest Heart', links her with the 'great-hearted' Goddess Athena.[84] Inanna is also a warrior goddess, and Athena, like Inanna, was originally a great cosmic Goddess of heaven and earth. Both are associated with serpents and birds,

---

78 Van der Kolk 2014: 38.
79 Shannon 2017a: 217.
80 Perera 1981: 31.
81 Perera 1981:92.
82 Shannon 2018.
83 Meador 2000: 174.
84 Solon 4.3, cited in Deacy 2008:78.

symbols of life, death and regeneration.[85] In the language of Armenian dance, the closing gesture of uplifted arms in the Dance of the Reed can also represent the holy mountain, associated since antiquity with both Inanna and Athena.

> *ancient city*
> *old reeds and young shoots shape you*
> *your heart, forged in plenty*
> *is a mountain of abundance*[86]

The dance circle itself is like Inanna's sacred storehouse, or Athena's circular temple, the *polis*, 'the round enclosure within which the women are safe.'[87] This *temenos* or sacred space allows the process of 'conscious healing dance,' to use Marcia Leventhal's term, to safely unfold.[88] Traditional circle dances have a natural ability to create this sacred space or safe container.[89] They 'provide a context for women to affirm and transmit pre-patriarchal values, such as the importance of community, mutual support, and shared leadership, within a circular, not a hierarchical structure.'[90]

We become priestesses of the dance, priestesses of Inanna. We ascend with her, redeeming our own underworld journeys and bringing her wisdom with us into the world.

---

85 Deacy 2008: 35, 41; Rigoglioso 2010: 24; Dexter 2010: 33.
86 Meador 2009: 50.
87 Shannon 2017a: 217.
88 Leventhal 2013.
89 Shannon 2014: 7.
90 Shannon 2016b.

References:

Barber, E. W. 2013. *The Dancing Goddesses*. New York: Norton.

Christ, C. P. 2017. 'The Mountain Mother: Reading the Language of the Goddess in the Symbols of Ancient Crete', on feminismandreligion.com, May 22 2017.

Deacy, S. 2008. *Athena*. London: Routledge.

Dexter, M. R. 2010. 'The Ferocious and the Erotic: "Beautiful" Medusa and the Neolithic Bird and Snake'. Journal of Feminist Studies in Religion, Vol. 26, No. 1, pp. 25-41.

Falkenstein, A. 1936. *Archaische Texte aus Uruk*. Berlin: Forschungsgemeinschaft. Zeichenliste, fig. 208. Cited in Meador 2000: 12.

Gimbutas, M. 1989. *The Language of the Goddess*. San Francisco: HarperCollins.

Leventhal, M. B. 2013. 'Bridge to the soul: The art of healing', Art 4 All People Interview Series, December. https://www.youtube.com/watch?v=Y9y3y4hhnWl. Accessed 11 February 2014.

Maxwell, G. 1933, reprinted 2003. *A Reed Shaken by the Wind: Travels Among the Marsh Arabs of Iraq*. London: Eland.

Meador, Betty De Shong 2000. *Inanna: Lady of Largest Heart*. Austin: University of Texas Press.

Meador, Betty De Shong 2009. *Princess, Priestess, Poet: The Sumerian Temple Hymns of Enheduanna*. Austin: University of Texas Press.

Perera, S. 1981. *Descent to the Goddess*. Toronto: Inner City Books.

Rigoglioso, M. 2009. *The Cult of Divine Birth in Ancient Greece*. New York: Palgrave Macmillan.

Rigoglioso, M. 2010. *Virgin Mother Goddesses of Antiquity*. New York: Palgrave Macmillan.

Shannon, L. 2014. 'Heiliger Raum und Körperhaltungen der Macht', Neue Kreise Ziehen, Heft 2-2014, 6-9.

Shannon, L. (ed.) 2016a. S*tring of Pearls: Celebrating 40 Years of Sacred Dance in the Findhorn Community*. Winchester: Sarsen Press.

Shannon, L. 2016b. 'Shared Leadership: The Hidden Treasure of Women's Ritual Dance', on feminismandreligion.com, November 1 2016.

Shannon, L. 2017a. 'Medusa and Athena: Ancient Allies in Healing Women's Trauma', in G. Livingstone, T. Hendren, and P. Daley (eds), *Revisioning Medusa: from Monster to Divine Wisdom*. Girl God Press, 206-222.

Shannon, L. 2017b. 'Symbols of the Goddess in Balkan Women's Dance' in *Dance, Movement & Spiritualities*, 4:1, 57-78, doi: 10.1386/dmas. 4.1.57_1.

Shannon, L. 2018. 'Opening Our Hearts Through Armenian Dance', on feminismandreligion.com, February 3 2018.

Silvermoon, S. 2012. 'The Original Venus – Goddess of Heaven, Earth and the Underworld', on goddessinspired.wordpress.com, May 13, 2012.

Solon. Fragment 4.3. Cited in Deacy, 2008.

Uždavinys, Algis. 2011. *Orpheus and the roots of Platonism*. London: Matheson Trust.

van der Kolk, B. 2014. *The Body Keeps the Score*. London: Penguin.

van Dijk, J. J. A. 'Les contacts ethniques dans la Mésopotamie et les syncrétismes de la religion sumérienne'. In *Syncretism*, edited by Sven S. Hartman. Stockholm: Almqvist & Wiksell, 1969, cited in Meador 2000:15.

Wosien, M-G. 2017. *Ariadne: Wandlungen im Tanz*. Dietikon, Switzerland: Metanoia Verlag.

For my Dumuzi
Tamara Albanna

Dumuzi
My Dumuzi
Without the betrayal

My soul has wandered aimlessly
Lifetime
After
Lifetime
Searching for you

I have descended to such depths
And seen unimaginable darkness
Without you

I would walk through it all
Again and again
Through the fire my darling
If only you would be there
Upon my ascent

Soon my love
I will be able to name you
And all will know why
I bloom once again

The Flight of Inanna
Liliana Kleiner

Painting from *The Song of Inanna*.

The Resurrection of Female Power
Trista Hendren

"What would our world look like if there were a rebirth of reverence for women, in all stages of life? How would we see ourselves if we were to revive the sacred feminine archetype?" -Amy Bammel Wilding[91]

Growing up in the Church, God was Male and I was shit.

I learned how to put myself last, in service to ALL—sacrificing myself daily in the service of His needs, whoever that man might be. The penis was my God, whether I recognized it or not then. There was no sacred masculine—and there still is not—because I cannot seem to recover that part of myself. Choking down dick will do that to a young woman.

Years later, I never understood my fascination with the Christa[92] figures, despite my absolute disgust with the Church.

If you're like me, what you remember most is the image of Jesus on the cross, ever-sacrificing—not the images of glory. Growing up in my particular denomination—we practiced a foot washing ceremony on Maundy Thursday.[93] It was my first glimpse of what a women's circle could entail—powerful!!!—and yet deeply

---

91 Bammel Wilding, Amy. *Wild & Wise: Sacred Feminine Meditations for Women's Circles & Personal Awakening.* Womancraft Publishing (October 9, 2017).
92 See "Christa" by Edwina Sandys (1975) and Arnfríður Guðmundsdóttir's paper, "When Christ becomes Christa."
Guðmundsdóttir, Arnfríður. "When Christ becomes Christa." Fyrirlestur í Wartburg Seminary Dubuque, Nóvember 2012.
93 Maundy Thursday is the Christian holy day falling on the Thursday before Easter, commemorating the foot washing and Last Supper of Jesus .

humbling to have someone else wash your feet and then to wash the feet of the woman next to you.

But that was a ritual saved for one night a year, and it would be years later before I discovered the power of women meeting together in circle regularly—with our own rituals.

As noted throughout this anthology, many females experience their first descent during girlhood.

> "Over time, the girl-child becomes disconnected from the 'home' within her. Caught in the swirls of others, twisted in the shapes of others, depleted by the demands of others, she becomes outer-directed and loses touch with herself. Her breath becomes shallow. She ignores her body. She looks to saviors outside of herself for salvation and validation, forgetting the rich resources within her."
> –Patricia Lynn Reilly[94]

It took me a long time to discover the lengths that patriarchy took to crucify me—or as it is often more politely phrased, to "clip my wings."

But I suppose if I am honest, it took even longer for me to realize that the act of clipping my wings could not keep me from resurrecting myself—and flying again.

You see, even if you clip a bird's wings, they will grow back— eventually. The bird just needs to learn how to fly.

All my life, I had been too focused on my cage. I did not even realize my wings had grown back and the door was unlocked. Hence, I never learned how to fly—it seemed beside the point.

---

94 Reilly, Patricia Lynn. *Be Full of Yourself!: The Journey from Self-Criticism to Self-Celebration.* Open Window Creations (April 1, 1998).

The easiest way to keep a woman caged is to make her believe she is powerless—and utterly incapable of flying on her own.

The simplest way to keep a woman on the cross is to convince her to keep her own nails in place—and even get her to nail them back into her own hands and feet when they come lose.

In my own life, I had been too focused on the systematic structures that hold women down. And believe me—they are there. We need to remove *all of them* so that girls do not continue to grow into women living in cages who *can't even feel* their wings.

Whether it be by incest, rape or other sexual abuse, physical, emotional or financial abuse, or the garden variety of subordination and submissiveness many of us are raised with—most females don't put up much of a fight anymore by adulthood. We often still feel those hands that held us down vividly, as if they were still there on our shoulders.

We are so disassociated with our bodies, we are barely even acquainted with them. We don't know our cycles, our vulvas, our breasts—or even our real food intake needs. Nothing. Nada. Zip. Most of us are completely divorced from ourselves before puberty.

I have come to strongly believe that no matter how much you *know* intellectually, you cannot claim your full power if you are disassociated from your body. And this self-hatred and unawareness of our bodies that is ingrained in girls from childhood must be stopped—and reversed in those of us who are older.

I didn't realize the full force of my own self-hatred until I watched Hannah Gadsby in *Nanette,* talking about her intense level of shame. Like most women, I was abused in a myriad of ways for the majority of my life. But it is that base level of indoctrination from birth that held me firmly in place in the underworld. As Gadsby howls so beautifully in her performance:

> "To be rendered powerless does not strip you of your humanity. Your resilience is your humanity... To yield and not break—that is *incredible* strength...
>
> There is no way, there is *no* way—anyone would dare test their strength out on me because you all know there is *nothing* stronger than a broken woman who has rebuilt herself."[95]

Patriarchy tends to go for the easy targets—namely, children—and women who have been sedated by the crushing weight of indoctrination and abuse.

I am currently remodeling an enormous, dilapidated house that I bought with my husband—and it has taught me a lot about myself. Among other things, I learned that all my life I had taken shortcuts that belittled my own best interests and growth.

My Norwegian husband is the slow and thorough type. I never have been that way. I always rush to get things done as soon as possible. We laugh at each other through this process as he insists on taking his own. sweet. time... filling holes, sanding, putting on primer—and then carefully applying 4 thin, even layers of paint.

My methods, if left to my own devices, would be exactly the opposite. I would just take a Super Soaker and squirt down all the walls until they were adequately drenched with a fresh, bright color. I think a lot of females work at speed-demon pace because we have too much on our plates—whereas men, statistically, have far more free time. We are used to taking the fastest way possible

---

[95] Gadsby, Hannah. *Nanette*. Netflix Original, 2018.

because we are constantly starved of time—especially time for ourselves.

What I realized during this process is that I never felt like I was worth it. I never thought I deserved any time spent on myself. I had spent my life giving away my hours, my days, my sovereignty and my-self.

Your home is a reflection of yourself in many ways, and there is no greater time in my life when I have felt this. We bought a once-grand old house that had been mistreated and abused for 40 years—much like I had been. The symbolism could not have been closer.

> "Say, who owns this house?
> It's not mine.
> This house is strange.
> Its shadows lie.
> Say, tell me, why does its lock fit my key?"
> -Toni Morrison, *Home*[96]

We are repairing the house as an investment—to restore some of what was destroyed by my previous husband's addictions. Mine was a messy 15-year descent, filled with every sort of loss. I have written entire books about my descent. I seem to have gotten stuck there somewhere along the way.

I expected my ascent to be much easier—but the truth is, it has been just as messy cleaning it up. Ascent is a *process,* which is why the story of Inanna is so important as a map for women.
There are no shortcuts during ascension. "Healing begins where the wound was made,"[97] as Alice Walker wrote. But returning to the wound often implies ripping off the band-aid—or the masks.

---

96 Morrison, Toni. Home. Vintage; (January 1, 2013).
97 Walker, Alice. *The Way Forward is With A Broken Heart. Ballantine* Books; 1st Ballantine Books ed edition (October 2, 2001).

When you are young, you can take shortcuts. If you have a fast metabolism and relative health, nothing really catches up with you for a while. You can still manage to look quite fabulous even if you've cried all night after not sleeping all week—and your life is completely falling apart.

After reaching 40, my health dwindled to the point where a large tumor formed in my abdomen. I couldn't get by with shortcuts anymore. I have had to look at myself a bit harder without the mask of fitting cultured beauty norms.

I was not eating well. I was not walking or doing yoga. I was not meeting in Women's Circles and I had isolated myself for the most part. I was not doing much of anything in regards to self-care that would ensure a good, long life. I didn't even take the time to breathe properly.

I stopped even brushing my hair most days, completely shunning any notion of beauty. I quit shaving or painting my toes, which will probably never be regular routines for me—but I also stopped my daily self-massages and other self-care. Perhaps I needed to do this for a time as I delved into rejecting patriarchal beauty standards—but for me, it became a regulatory function of my self-hatred. I was not worth getting dressed up for. I stopped wearing clothes and jewelry I enjoyed. I did not let myself take pleasure in my appearance and adornments. This all seemed fussy, unnecessary—selfish even.

By subverting the Inanna myth and inserting Christ as Savior instead, patriarchy did a pretty good job of mind-fucking the world. We are taught the opposite of Goddess values in the Christian narrative. As Monica Sjöö and Barbara Mor wrote in *The Great Cosmic Mother,* "The patriarchal God has only one commandment: Punish life for being what it is. The Goddess also only has one commandment: Love life for what it is."[98]

Inanna dresses herself elaborately for Her descent. Everything was (willingly) taken from Her, as it was from me rather begrudgingly. What I forgot though—without the myth of Inanna directing my own life—is that *all* was returned to her.

I did not need to continue to walk around in tattered clothes my entire life like my image of a crucified Jesus returning from the grave. My particular image of Jesus was nearly always that of him suffering immensely on the cross for my sins. Even more than 20 years after leaving the church, I am not sure I ever really got over my feelings of unworthiness.

I talked about self love—and even co-wrote a book about it. But my affection for myself was weak. As Toni Morrison wrote, "Love is or it ain't. Thin love ain't love at all."[99]

I was still putting absolutely everyone—even random people on the internet—in front of myself—long after most toxic and abusive people were completely out of my life. No one was asking me to do this, or even expecting me to do it. In fact, I had the most supportive people in the world surrounding me and rooting me on.

My internalized oppression was strong. And there is no blame in that. We indoctrinate girls from birth to hate themselves and put themselves dead-last. Arnfríður Guðmundsdóttir wrote that "Women's sufferings have been justified by appealing to the salvific significance of their suffering."[100]

---

98 Sjöö, Monica and Mor, Barbara. *The Great Cosmic Mother: Rediscovering the Religion of the Earth*. HarperOne; 2nd edition, 1987.
99 Morrison, Toni. *Beloved*. Vintage; Reprint edition (June 8, 2004).
100 Guðmundsdóttir, Arnfríður. "When Christ becomes Christa." Fyrirlestur í Wartburg Seminary Dubuque, Nóvember 2012.

In order for us to rise, we must shred these beliefs. And then we must actively dissolve their hooks in every area of our lives.

> "This Second Coming is not a return of Christ but a new arrival of female presence, once strong and powerful, but enchained since the dawn of patriarchy. Only this arrival can liberate the memory of Jesus from enchainment to the role of "mankind's most illustrious scapegoat." The arrival of women means the removal of the primordial victim, "the Other," because of whom "the Son of God had to die." When no longer condemned to the role of "savior," perhaps Jesus can be recognizable as a free man. It is only female pride and self-affirmation that can release the memory of Jesus from its destructive uses and can free freedom to be contagious. The Second Coming, then, means that the prophetic dimension in the symbol of the great Goddess—later reduced to the "Mother of God"—is the key to salvation from servitude to structures that obstruct human becoming." -Mary Daly[101]

I thought I had embraced these words full-heartedly. Intellectually I had. But internally I was still doing the little things every single day that said *I hate myself.*

It is not always the big things... oftentimes it is the small things that are too minuscule to even seem important. But when they become daily habits, they can take over everything else. They can rob us of our joy—and even our lives.
As Sandra Heimann explained:

> "Goddess was weakened by fragmentation; gods gained power by assembling fragments; they cobbled together a "monotheistic" god from stolen goddess parts."[102]

---

[101] Daly, Mary. *Beyond God the Father: Toward a Philosophy of Women's Liberation.* Beacon Press; Revised edition (June 1, 1993).

Likewise, patriarchy teaches women to fragment *themselves* to complete the destruction of all that is female.

And no matter how you do female, you will do it wrong.

Hannah Gadsby describes it as being "Incorrectly female."[103] Lesbians are perhaps the ultimate expression of that. However, any female who does not perform the patriarchal mandate perfectly (which is impossible, because it was *designed* to be unattainable) pays for it deeply. One reason men worked so hard to destroy the Goddess through their man-made religions is that She inspires women to claim their power through Her images and stories.

> "Inanna represents the nondomesticated woman, and exemplifies all the fear and attraction that such a woman elicits. She is the exception to the rule, the woman who does not behave in societally approved ways, the goddess who models the crossing of gender lines and the danger that this presents."[104]

We must reclaim our nondomesticated and wild selves in all their glory.

I have been learning Norwegian the last three years, which is a humbling process at best. It's frustrating to talk like a 2-year-old in your forties. I find myself questioning myself even in English, looking up words I have known for decades to check their spelling or meaning. I realized in the process of writing this that I have been afraid to be child-like in my speaking of this new language—

---

102 Heimann, Sandra. *The Biography of Goddess Inanna; Indomitable Queen of Heaven, Earth and Almost Everything: Her Story Is Women's Story.* BalboaPress (September 29, 2016).
103 Gadsby, Hannah. *Nanette*. Netflix Original, 2018.
104 Frymer-Kensky, Tikva. *In the Wake of the Goddesses: Women, Culture and the Biblical Transformation of Pagan Myth.* Ballantine Books (February 10, 1993).

which has ultimately prevented me from speaking it well. The wild woman is child-like in her fearlessness.

Judy Grahn wrote that,

> "Inanna attains laws of the cosmos in the myth, Inanna Meets the God of Wisdom, a story that helps teach women that **power is paradoxical**, belongs to them, and involves struggle."[105]

I had to look up the meaning of paradoxical because the enigma of learning another language is that you both forget your own language at times—and, ultimately, (re)learn it better. The Webster online dictionary tells us that paradoxical means, "seemingly absurd or self-contradictory."

That hits home for me, because the idea of my own power has always seemed completely unattainable, and the idea of expressing it somehow feels utterly self-contradictory.

Starhawk wrote:

> "The Goddess falls in love with Herself, drawing forth her own emanation, which takes on a life of its own. Love of self for self is the creative force of the universe. Desire is the primal energy, and that energy is erotic: the attraction of lover to beloved, of planet to star, the lust of electron for proton. Love is the glue that holds the world together."[106]

---

[105] Grahn, Judy . (2010). "Ecology of the erotic in a myth of Inanna." International Journal of Transpersonal Studies, 29(2), 58–67.. International Journal of Transpersonal Studies, 29 (2).

[106] Starhawk, *The Spiral Dance: A Rebirth of the Ancient Religions of the Great Goddess*. HarperOne; Annual, Subsequent edition (September 22, 1999).

We must learn to fall in love with ourselves as well. Doing so is difficult: It flies in the face of every cultural norm for females anywhere in the world. But, small steps and Goddess-willing, I am taking the plunge.

From here on out, I put myself first. I reclaim my sovereignty. I will eat a proper breakfast, do yoga and meditate before I even open my laptop or check my phone. I will meet in circle face-to-face with other women regularly. I will eat lunch, make fresh vegetable juice and drink my homemade broth daily. I will be out in nature every day, touching Mother earth with my feet and hands.

I will take the time to do the sanding, mend the gaps, apply the primer and apply each layer of paint carefully—to create not only a beautiful picture, but to build a solid and magnificent life.

I invite you to join me.

We have been focused on patriarchal crucifixion stories for too long. When we put our own stories back together, we put our lives back together—and we reclaim our power. As Hannah Gadsby says, "You learn from the part of the story you focus on."[107] We must reclaim the resurrection of Goddess—and use Her stories to learn how to ascend in our lives.

May the legend of Inanna—and the tales of ascension by Her daughters—inspire global transformation that will resurrect female power everywhere.

---

107 Gadsby, Hannah. *Nanette*. Netflix Original, 2018.

List of Contributors

Amanda Lee Morris is a clinical social worker, ordained minister, and initiated high priestess who lives in North Carolina where she enjoys a life full of love.

Annelinde Metzner has devoted her creative life in both music composition and poetry to the reemergence of the Goddess. She has composed solo art songs honoring the Divine Feminine, as well as a book of choral pieces for the Goddesses of Europe, Africa and the Middle East called "Lady of Ten Thousand Names." Her poetry can be found in the *We'Moon Datebook* as well as in *Goddess Pages* of Glastonbury, and at her blog, *Annelinde's World* (http://annelindesworld.blogspot.com/). She lives in Black Mountain, North Carolina where she directs two choirs, teaches music, and worships the Goddess in the natural world all around her.

Annie Finch is a poet, writer, speaker, workshop leader, and performer of poetry and ritual. Her writings include *Spells: New and Selected Poems,* the abortion epic *Among the Goddesses*, and the forthcoming *The Witch in You: Five Directions to Your Inner Goddess.* Annie has received the Robert Fitzgerald Award and the Sarasvati Award for Poetry from the Association for the Study of Women and Mythology. For Annie's Spells inspirational newsletter, Healing Rhythms workshops, retreats, rituals, conferences, talks, and other events, please visit www.anniefinch.com

Arna Baartz (cover artist and contributor) is a painter, writer/poet, martial artist, educator and mother to eight fantastic children. She has been expressing herself creatively for 44 years and finds it to be her favourite way of exploring her inner being enough to evolve positively in an externally focused world. Arna's artistic and literary expression is her creative perspective of the stories she observes playing out around her. Claims to fame: Arna has been selected for major art prizes and won a number of awards, published books and (her favourite) was used as a 'paintbrush' at the age of two by well known Australian artist John Olsen. Arna lives and works from her bush studio in the Northern Rivers, NSW Australia. Her website is www.artofkundalini.com

Benedetta Crippa is a graphic designer based in Stockholm with an MFA in Visual Communication from Konstfack. Her degree work, *World of Desire,* is an artist's book exploring plurality and visual democracy. She is interested in the ways in which decoration, emotion and compassion can expand contemporary design practices. www.instagram.com/benedetta.crippa

Carolina Miranda, OCT, M.Ed. is an Educator certified by the Ontario College of Teachers, and she holds a Masters of Education from Nipissing University. She is one of the main organizers of the Waterloo Region Women's March, in Ontario, Canada as well as the creator and co-founder of Feminine Harbor. She immigrated to Canada from Brazil in 2003 and has since developed strong ties with the Waterloo Region. In 2004 she became one of the very first ensemble actors for the internationally acclaimed theatre company The MT Space, directed then by Lebanese-Canadian director Majdi Bou-Matar. She is a writer, and some of her most recent essays and poetry can be found in the *Anthology of Social Justice and Intersectional Feminisms*, organized by Dr. Katrina Sark, and which has officially launched on International Women's Day 2018 in Victoria, BC. Most importantly, however, she is a single mother of two incredible little girls who inspire her daily to become not only a better person but to leave behind a better world. Equity, Diversity, and Inclusion are not just aspects of her job, but how she authentically experiences the world through her relationships and family ties.

Carolyn Lee Boyd is a New Englander who writes fiction, poetry, essays, and memoirs celebrating the spirituality and creativity in women's everyday lives. Over the past three decades, she has published in women's and feminist literary, art, and spirituality magazines, both in print and online. You may read her musings and published writings, as well as find out where to purchase her new novel or download a free copy, by going to her blogsite, http://goddessinateapot.com. When she isn't writing, she grows herbs and native flowers, raises a family, and props up her constantly falling-down Victorian house.

Chantal Khoury (b 1986) is from New Brunswick, Canada but has been based in Montreal since 2006. She obtained her BFA with distinction from Concordia University (2012) and has been developing her practice ever since. Ongoing themes in her work address the female 'self,' where women's identities are often repurposed and re-imagined. She examines her own childhood, her place in the Lebanese diaspora and her relationship to the Canadian landscape. These subjects act as a point of departure and her narrative speaks as both 'tourist' and 'resident.' She has exhibited widely across Canada, including a solo exhibition at the University of New Brunswick, the Orillia Museum of Art & History, and a solo exhibition in Montreal. She has taught at the Beaverbrook Art Gallery and her work is found in private and public collections, including the permanent collection of the University of New Brunswick.

Daphne Moon has studied many forms of ceremony and circle and draws inspiration most directly from Hindu scripture, Yogic teachings, Dianic circles, and Lakota practices. Her ceremony allows for many levels of participation, giving each individual the opportunity to join or witness at their level of comfort and desire.

She has been practicing yoga since a car accident in 2006 and has been teaching since 2012. Because of her personal struggles with chronic pain from injuries, depression and anxiety since childhood, surviving domestic violence, and rebirthing herself through motherhood, her teaching style is nurturing and gentle while creating strength and stability.

Her Sacred Dream is to open a self-sustaining community of spiritual guides, health and wellness practitioners, and experts on sustainable food and energy production that acts as a hub of learning, growth, and green living.

DeAnna L'am is fondly known as 'Womb Visionary.' DeAnna is a motivational speaker, workshop leader, author, and a trailblazer who defined the last missing pieces in women's psyche today: harnessing the spiritual forces hidden in both Menstruation and Menopause. DeAnna has been leading workshops, and certifying facilitators, nationally and internationally for over 30 years.
She is author of: *Becoming Peers - Mentoring Girls Into Womanhood* and *A Diva's Guide to Getting Your Period*. Founder of: Red Tents In Every Neighborhood – Global Network; Red Moon School of Empowerment for Women & Girls™; WOMB WISDOM Tribe, and International Red Tent Day (celebrated globally on November 8). Visit DeAnna at: www.deannalam.com

Rev. DiAnna Ritola is an ordained Interfaith Minister and Dianic Wiccan Priestess who works at the intersections of spirituality and sexuality as they come alive in intimate relationships. She has been speaking, counseling, and teaching about shame, sexuality, body image, and sex and religion since 2008. She is passionate about healing the grief and wounds we carry around that impact our relationships with ourselves, others, and the Divine. DiAnna advocates for unpacking the baggage of shame surrounding sexuality and desire. She believes that the more we talk about our bodies, sex, and sexuality with honesty, humor, and compassion, the better able we are to celebrate the fact that sexual intimacy can be a fantastic athletic adventure, a fun and giggly interlude, as well as one of the most spiritual journeys we can undertake.
She works with individuals, couples, and groups.
www.DiAnnaRitola.com

Donna Snyder founded the Tumblewords Project in 1995 and continues to organize its free weekly workshop series and other events. She has three collections of poetry published by various independent presses. Her poem, "Seeking Oracles," was previously published in *BorderSenses*, Volume 21, and included in *Paso del Norte Poets Sing*.

Genevieve Deven walks the sacred spiral of life as a mother, healer and artist. By stepping onto the path of the Priestess, she could no longer deny the Dark Goddess her dance. That dance led her on a journey through the depths of heartache to the heights of self-empowerment, reclaiming sovereignty and wholeness, respecting both the light and the shadow. Genevieve strives to be a source of empowerment for women and girls to recognize their intrinsic self-worth and their wild, wise woman within. She inconspicuously celebrates the Goddess in every woman and the Divine Masculine in every man while living in a conservative, Christian community of Southern California. Thus, bringing the essence of the Goddess and earth-based spirituality into the mostly unlikely of places.

Glenys Livingstone, Ph.D. has been on a Goddess path since 1979. She is the author of *PaGaian Cosmology: Re-inventing Earth-based Goddess Religion*, which fuses the indigenous traditions of Old Europe with scientific theory, feminism and a poetic relationship with place. She lives in the Blue Mountains of Australia where she has facilitated Seasonal ceremony for over two decades, taught classes and mentored apprentices. In 2014, Glenys co-facilitated the Mago Pilgrimage to Korea with Dr. Helen Hwang. Glenys is a contributor to the recently published *Foremothers of Women's Spirituality: Elders and Visionaries* edited by Miriam Robbins Dexter and Vicki Noble. She has recently produced a set of meditation CDs which are available at her website: http://pagaian.org/pagaian-prayers-invoking-her/, along with her book http://pagaian.org/book/

Hayley Arrington earned her M.A. in women's spirituality from the Institute of Transpersonal Psychology, where she wrote her thesis on Celtic sun goddesses. Her interests include mythology and folklore as sacred text, writing essays, fiction and poetry, and discovering women's myriad ways of knowing. Her writings have appeared in *Eternal Haunted Summer*, *Goddess When She Rules: Expressions by Contemporary Women*, *SageWoman* Magazine, and elsewhere. She is a devotee of Hera and a member of Twilight Spiral Coven. Hayley was born and raised in the greater Los Angeles area, where she still lives with her husband, David and their son, Stephen.

Hazel DaHealer is a Dianic Priestess who is Mom to an adult daughter and cats. She earned a degree in Criminal Justice and Public Service. Hazel enjoys spending time with her loved ones, tending her plants and crystals, and hanging out at the water's edge by a fire. She serves her community through readings and public rituals.

Artist, author, mystic and consciousness counselor, **Heather Mendel** was born and educated in South Africa. Following on the success of her 2016 book and deck, *The Sacred Mandala Tarot: mystery, mindfulness and manifestation*, comes her 2018 project: *The Magic Moon Lenormand Oracle* and the accompanying book, *The Oracle Speaks*. Her earlier books are: *Dancing In The Footsteps of Eve: retrieving the healing gift of the Sacred Feminine through Myth and Mysticism*, published by O Books, 2009 and her 1995 feminist hagaddah:*Towards Freedom; a feminist haggadah for men and women* for which she wrote and typeset the text and hand-drew the illustrations, border design and cover. Believing the future is not prescribed, and using her oracle decks as a consciousness counselor, Heather offers (in person or via email, phone or Skype), one-on-one intuitive readings that focus on the beliefs held that profoundly influence expectations. With awareness, we are empowered able to make the most informed choices possible, manifesting our desired future in a consciously evolving manner.

Iriome R. Martín Alonso is an anthropology and performing arts student, born in the Canary Islands, Spain (1996). Coming from a strictly Catholic family in which it was usual for women to become nuns, she changed Her faith at the age of thirteen- After seven years moving with the cycles of the Wheel of the Year consciously, she's currently taking face-to-face training to become a Priestess of the Goddess at the Goddess Temple of Madrid.

Iyana Rashil prefers evolutionary violet or futuristic mauve colored lenses to look at life through. Her degree in Human Development grounds her. Interlace it with a love for science fiction, universal spiritual paths and consciousness curiosities and an Evolutionary Visionary Spiritualist colors the pages of her prose. She blogs her perspectives at thenewerview.com and her recently self-published works are *Amour Desiré: Aphrodite's Dance with the Colors of Higher Love* and *Number Eleven Authentic Numerology Messages.*

Jaclyn Cherie has her roots in Upstate New York. She is an Author, Witch, Feminist and Luciferian. The Owner and Creatrix of The Nephilim Rising strives to tell raw, real stories of Magick, the human condition, Sacred Sex, Women's Issues and her favorite topic, rebellion. Preferring the Shadows to the Light, her Magick and writing reflect this; it is in the Darkness that she found her true form. Her written works originate from the watery depths of her Cancerian Soul and chronicle her cyclical death and rebirth from the Womb of the Dragon.

K. A. Laity is an award-winning author, scholar and critic. Her books include *How to Be Dull, White Rabbit, Dream Book, A Cut-Throat Business, Lush Situation, Owl Stretching, Unquiet Dreams, Chastity Flame,* and *Pelzmantel.* She has edited *My Wandering Uterus, Respectable Horror, Weird Noir, Noir Carnival* and *Drag Noir*, plus written many short stories, scholarly essays, songs, and more. Follow her on Twitter and Facebook or at KALaity.com

Laura Shannon has researched and taught traditional circle dances for more than thirty years, and is considered to be one of the 'grandmothers' of the worldwide Sacred / Circle Dance movement. Through extensive research in Balkan villages and wide teaching experience, Laura has pioneered a new understanding of traditional women's dances as active tools for spiritual development. Originally trained in Intercultural Studies and Dance Movement Therapy, Laura is currently pursuing an M.A. in Myth, Cosmology and the Sacred at Canterbury Christ Church University in England. She gives workshops, trainings and performances in more than twenty countries, and her numerous articles on dance have been published in many languages. She is founding director of the Athena Institute for Womens' Dance and Culture and a regular contributor to *Feminism and Religion*. In between her travels, Laura resides in Canterbury, Findhorn and Greece. www.laurashannon.net

Laura Tempest Zakroff is a professional artist, author, dancer, and designer. She holds a BFA from RISD (The Rhode Island School of Design) and her artwork has received awards and honors worldwide. Her work embodies myth and the esoteric through her drawings and paintings, jewelry, talismans, and other designs. Laura has been a practicing Modern Traditional Witch for over two decades and revels in the intersection of her various paths with witchcraft. She blogs for Patheos as A *Modern Traditional Witch*, Witches & Pagans as *Fine Art Witchery,* and contributes to *The Witches' Almanac, Ltd.* Laura is the author of *Sigil Witchery: A Witch's Guide to Crafting Magick Symbols, The Witch's Cauldron: The Craft, Lore & Magick of Ritual Vessels, The Witch's Altar (co-authored with Jason Mankey - November 2018)* and *Weave The Liminal: Living Modern Traditional Witchcraft (January 2019).* Find out more at www.lauratempestzakroff.com

Lennée Reid is trying to make sense of it all and find peace. They facilitate meditation and speak about all kinds of social justice issues including race, feminism, poverty, being a survivor and the environment. Lennée has featured and slammed across the USA and is published in; *Farm to Table, The UPS Dirt! Project, Creative Colloquy, The Bus Stop Project, Tattoosday, Lost Tower, Panegyria, Works In Progress, Spectrum Women, Strangefoot*, and her chapbook *Universal State of Mind*, published by The Girl God. She was The Olympia Peoples Mic first WOWPS representative, opened for Pussy Riot, was heard on Paradigms, Tell It Slant, and Wheel of Wonder.

Her spoken word poetry album *The Second Coming of Matriarchy* is available at lenneereid.bandcamp.com
Follow her @lenneereid and at mamamystic.wordpress.com

Liliana Kleiner Ph.D. is a visual artist born in Argentina and raised in Israel. She divides her time living and working in Jerusalem and in North and South America.

Liliana is known for her visionary oil paintings and her earthy woodcuts which convey her vision of the "Spirit of the Earth." Her work is Visual Poetry from a Feminine Spiritual perspective.

Liliana creates her own organic hand-made paper, and has published two art books—*The Song of Lilith* (2007) and *The Song of Songs*, Jerusalem (2010). She has produced art films—*Lilith and the Tree* (1993) and *Lesbian Tango* (2006) and works with Performance arts and dance.

In addition to her career as an artist , Liliana has a Ph.D. in Clinical Psychology, and specializes in Jungian Dream Analysis.

Her work is in galleries and private collections in America and Israel, and can be seen on her site: www.lilianakleiner.com

Lyn Thurman is the author of *The Inner Goddess Revolution* and *Goddess Rising*, and creator of the *Sea Whispers* oracle. A witch and pagan priestess, she infuses the gifts of the goddess with modern life to guide and inspire others. Lyn lives on the south coast of England with her family and a ridiculous amount of tarot decks. You can find more about her at www.lynthurman.com.

Melanie Miner is the Founder and Director of Chrysalis Woman. She is an Ordained High Priestess, Queen Activation Coach and Self-Care Specialist who elevates old-world light WORKERS into new paradigm light LEADERS. She offers workbooks, road maps, initiations and coaching programs on the Queen Archetype and Light Leader Sovereignty. She can be reached at www.chrysaliswoman.com

Melissa Stratton Pandina is an artist whose work has been internationally published and sold. Twenty years ago, she delved into Shamanism after encountering a chronic illness. Her work is inspired by Irish spirituality, Huna, Folkloric Magic and Animism. She is currently co-creating the Oracle of the Seer. Check out her work at www.Deshria.com.

Miriam Robbins Dexter holds a Ph.D. in ancient Indo-European languages, archaeology, and comparative mythology, from UCLA. Her first book, *Whence the Goddesses: A Source Book* (1990), in which she translated texts from thirteen languages, was used for courses she taught at UCLA for a decade and a half. She completed and supplemented the final book of Marija Gimbutas, *The Living Goddesses* (1999). Her 2010 book, coauthored with Victor Mair, *Sacred Display: Divine and Magical Female Figures of Eurasia*, won the 2012 Association for the Study of Women and Mythology Sarasvati award for best nonfiction book on women and mythology. In 2013, Miriam and Victor published a new monograph, "Sacred Display: New Findings" in the University of Pennsylvania's online series, *Sino-Platonic Papers*. With Vicki Noble, she edited the anthology, *Foremothers of the Women's Spirituality Movement: Elders and Visionaries* (2015); winner of the Susan Koppelman award for best edited feminist anthology, 2016. Miriam is the author of more than 30 scholarly articles and 11 encyclopedia articles on ancient female figures. She has edited and co-edited 16 scholarly volumes. For 13 years, she taught courses in Latin, Greek, and Sanskrit languages in the department of Classics at USC. She has guest-lectured at the New Bulgarian

University (Sophia, Bulgaria) and "Alexandru Ioan Cuza" University (Iaşi, Moldavia, Romania).

Molly Remer has been gathering the women to circle, sing, celebrate, and share since 2008. She plans and facilitates women's circles, seasonal retreats, Pink Tents, Red Tents, and family ceremonies in rural Missouri and teaches online courses in Red Tent facilitation and Practical Priestessing. She is a priestess who holds MSW, M.Div, and D.Min degrees and she wrote her dissertation about contemporary priestessing. Molly and her husband Mark co-create Story Goddesses, mini goddesses, goddess grids, and ceremony kits at Brigid's Grove. Molly is the author of *Womanrunes, Earthprayer*, and *The Red Tent Resource Kit* and she writes about thealogy, nature, practical priestessing, and the goddess at brigidsgrove.com

Nina Erin Hofmeijer is a writer, mother, healer and mostly-gentle truth-teller living in Eugene, OR.

Nuit Moore is a priestess whose work and temple serve the Goddess and Her return to the collective consciousness, focusing especially on the empowerment of women, the return of the Goddess temple, and the mana and medicine of her path and teachings. Although she comes from mystic traditions from both sides of her bloodline, she began her personal path as priestess in the Dianic and Wise Woman traditions, and is also an ordained priestess with the Fellowship of Isis. She is a lineage carrier and has walked the path of this work since her earliest memories. Nuit has offered classes and ceremony on female shamanism, women's red moon mysteries, the Dark Goddess, sacred sexuality, the trance arts, pharmakeia, women's healing arts, serpent/shakti power, crystals and crystal grids, ceremonial movement and sound and ritual theater, etc. for almost 25 years and travels frequently bringing temple and ceremony to festivals and communities. She has been a visionary and teacher of the menstrual mysteries and eco-menstruation movement since 1991 and is a long standing weaver of the Red Tent web. In addition, much of her work as an eco-feminist activist is in connection with her teachings of holistic menstruation and women's sexual health empowerment. Nuit is also a performance artist/sacred dancer, ceremonial visual artist, spoken word siren, temple arts empress, and founder of the Ishtar Noir Ritual Theater collective—and is the creatrix of Shakti Goddess Arts (www.shaktistudios.etsy.com) which carries her ceremonial offerings, herbals, menstrual sea sponges, yoni eggs, crystals, sacred art, and some of her written work, including *Ragtime Revolution* and *The Ruby in the Lotus*. Her website can be found at www.scarletshakti.com and she is also on Facebook at: Nuit Moore, The Scarlet Shakti.

Pat Daly (editor) is a mother of three daughters and proud grandma. A published author / writer on career and job search issues, Pat lives in Portland, Oregon.

Patricia Ballentine Artist, Author, Priestess, Death Midwife, Ordained Minister.

Patricia was first called by the Goddess in 1996. She is known to many as an integrated artist. With an engineering background and over 40 years of experience as an industrial designer she consciously blends mind and heart in all of her creative expressions.

Patricia is the founder of the Temple of the Creative Flame, an interfaith Pagan community. A temple for thinkers and lovers of life, building bridges through ceremony, ritual and dialogue within safe and sacred space, all are welcome who come with open minds and open hearts.

A practitioner of the deepest magic, which is the transformation of self, Patricia's focus is on the expansion of beauty, integration, unity and wholeness. Her spiritual life focuses on the ancient wheel of the year and Nature is her church.

A graduate of Ohio State University, **Psyche North Torok** is a writer and lover of words, language, and Nature. Her poems have appeared in *Common Ground Review*, *Mountain Astrologer*, and various collections including the Grayson Books anthology, *Forgotten Women*. She lives and works in Columbus, Ohio.

Sinem Alev Koca, PA and philosophy student, advocates radical self-love for women to heal in their strides. When she does not write, she enjoys volunteering or spending time with her family.

Sofia Wren Nitchie graduated Bryn Mawr '09, and Loyola University Baltimore '18 with an M.A. in Spiritual and Pastoral Care. As a singer-songwriter, she has sang on stages in 3 states, and as a writer she shares inspiration to help her tribe embrace their Creative Power. Sofia does a lot: volunteers as a Spiritual Director, holds a license in massage, writes professionally, and helps writers and creatives to make progress and put themselves out there in a bigger way. Since 2011 she's worked with numerous women, including writers and entrepreneurs helping them always know what to do next because they can hear their intuition and trust it. Everyone can create and be intuitive. Take the next step on your path as a spiritual creator if you want to get your experience and wisdom out to the world in the form of a book. Sofiawren.com

Susan Morgaine is a Daughter of the Goddess, Witch, Writer, Healer, Yogini. She is a certified Kundalini Yoga teacher; a Reiki Master, who also works with chakras to clear the chakras; She priestesses a Red Tent in southern MA (US), as well as teaching Goddess Spirituality workshops. She is a writer whose work can be found in The Girl God Anthologies, *Whatever Works: Feminists of Faith Speak* and *Jesus, Mohammad and the Goddess*, as well as Mago Publications *She Rises, Volume 2*, and *Seasons of the Goddess*. She has also been published in *SageWoman* magazine and is a monthly columnist in PaganPages.org. She is the author of *My Name is Isis, the Egyptian Goddess,* one in the series of the *My*

Name Is... children's books published by The Girl God Publications. She is a Certified Women's Empowerment Coach/Facilitator through Imagine A Woman International founded by Patricia Lynn Reilly. She is a member of the Sisterhood of Avalon. Her website is MysticalShores.wordpress.com and she can be reached at MysticalShores@gmail.com.

Talia Segal is best known for the powerful world building that she brings to writing fantasy fiction, and has a fashion blog with international readership (wildroma.wordpress.com). She played roller derby under the name Riot Gere, reads and writes graphic novels, designs knitting patterns, and obeys the directives of her cat. More of her writing can be found at Patreon.com/taliasegal

Tamara Albanna has always been connected to the Goddess, even when she didn't realize it. As a Doula and Childbirth Educator, she witnessed divinity first hand through other women. Now as a writer, Reiki healer and Tarot reader, she hopes to help others overcome their difficult pasts while healing with the Divine Mother. Tamara currently resides in Europe with her family.

Tara Reynolds creates beautiful art that transports the viewer into another world. She believes art should serve as an escape from the ordinary and the mundane. That it should spark imagination and creativity. Tara gets her inspiration from nature, myth and her own personal spirituality. All of her art is created with love in her studio in sunny Orlando, Florida. To see more of Tara's art, please visit www.etsy.com/shop/TaraFineArt

Trista Hendren (editor and contributor) is the creator of *The Girl God* series. She lives in Bergen, Norway with her family. You can read more about her projects at www.thegirlgod.com

Singer, Songwriter, Hugger of Trees: **Vicki Scotti** has been writing songs, singing, and playing guitar since the age of 12. When not playing music for the Goddess, she works as a Registered Nurse in a gated community. She is a founding member of the folk duo 'Hecate's Wheel.' Her songs are invocations to the Goddess and dedicated to the divine feminine. Many of her songs are about the healing and transformative power of dark Goddess energy. The piece submitted for consideration "Inanna Blue," is a song from the band's first self-titled CD "Hecate's Wheel."

Praise for Re-Visioning Medusa

"Gifted Women's Spirituality poets, artists, and scholars create a fascinating portal to open our understanding of Medusa and her powers, to protect and heal, and also to destroy. Medusa's angry fierceness — that opposes social oppression and other violations of the matristic values of community, cooperation, and caring — will find a resonance among spiritually awakening readers for facing the political challenges of today."
-Mara Lynn Keller, PhD, Professor of Philosophy, Religion and Women's Spirituality, California Institute of Integral Studies

"I welcome *Re-visioning Medusa: from Monster to Divine Wisdom* wholeheartedly. Medusa unfolds the original vision of the female divine. Calling her a rebel underestimates her power. In short, the symbol of Medusa embodies Goddess Feminism, Activism, and Spirituality. Together with women, Medusa is ever present in the intergalactic journey of the Great Goddess."
-Helen Hye-Sook Hwang, Ph.D., author of *The Mago Way: Re-discovering Mago, the Great Goddess from East Asia*

"This deeply felt, thought and illustrated anthology asks us to imagine, know, feel, and face Medusa. This ancient goddess is not the monster to be slain by a patriarchal hero, but the face of the Earth and of wisdom. The diverse offerings in this wonderful anthology lead readers to knowledge, through study as well as dreams, art, and storytelling. It is a very fine and compelling read and also a glorious guide for getting down to the Earth wisdom so direly needed in these times."
-Jane Caputi, Ph.D, Professor, Center for Women, Gender and Sexuality Studies, Communication & Multimedia, Florida Atlantic University

Praise for The Girl God

"*The Girl God*: a picture book to show girls that god can be a girl, god is inside, god is an idea, a positive action or good deed, god is open to creative interpretation and should be about everyone. A great book to dispel the myth that god is male with wonderful illustrations by Elisabeth Slettnes. Empowerment for our girl children." –a girl's guide to taking over the world

"Read this book to your daughters and your grand daughters, and perhaps they will never doubt the validity of their inner voice. Read it to yourself to remind you of your own. Read it and weep. Read it and heal. Read it and smile with the relief that someone finally had the courage to tell our girls that God is not just for their brothers and their fathers. Walk away knowing that the God of Abraham, Isaac and Jacob is equally the God of Sarah, Rebekah and Rachel. But most importantly, walk away knowing there is a Girl God inside you too."
–Monette Chilson, author of *Sophia Rising*

"A deceptively simple story about a whimsical young girl named Helani Claire, who would make Emily Dickinson smile as she deconstructs the patriarchal god of her father with the bluntness of a child. Akin to: If Kate Chopin was still alive, writing (and self-publishing) children's books. Elisabeth Slettnes' colorful paintings are feasts for the spirit, as are the addition of selected quotes and poems. Wisdom abounds." –*Philadelphia Weekly*

"This book will be one I treasure, for it is rare indeed—the articulation of the divine feminine for both children and adults, a bridge between our spiritual beginning and our spiritual future, a spark for the reawakening of humanity."
–Elizabeth Hall Magill, author of *Defining Sexism*

Stay Tuned!

The next anthologies in this series are:

On the Wings of Isis: A Woman's Path to Sovereignty

Warrior Queen: Answering the Call of The Morrigan

Anthologies and children's books on Willendorf, Aradia, Mary, Kali and Kuan Yin are also in the works.

See a complete list of books at www.thegirlgod.com

Made in the USA
Coppell, TX
15 July 2021